THE POETRY OF
RESISTANCE

THE POETRY OF
RESISTANCE

Seamus Heaney and the Pastoral Tradition

SIDNEY BURRIS

OHIO UNIVERSITY PRESS

ATHENS

for my mother,
and my father, *in memoriam*

Ohio University Press books are printed on acid-free paper ∞

© Copyright 1990 by Sidney Burris
Printed in the United States of America
All rights reserved

Library of Congress Cataloging-in-Publication Data

Burris, Sidney, 1953–
The poetry of resistance : Seamus Heaney and the pastoral tradition /
Sidney Burris.
p.   cm.
ISBN 0-8214-0951-4
1. Heaney, Seamus—Criticism and interpretation. 2. Political poetry,
English—History and criticism. 3. Pastoral poetry, English—History and
criticism. 4. Northern Ireland in literature. I. Title.
PR6058.E2Z56   1990
821'.914—dc20   89-25502
                                                                          CIP

Contents

Preface

In July 1985, I received a letter from an inmate at H.M.P. Maze in County Antrim, Northern Ireland. He had been arrested in 1977 and eventually sentenced to life imprisonment for the murder of a British policeman. At the time of his arrest he was nineteen; I had begun my correspondence with him in 1983, when he was twenty-six years old. In 1972, when my correspondent had reached his mid-teens, Seamus Heaney resigned his teaching appointment at Queen's University, Belfast, and moved south with his family to County Wicklow in the Republic of Ireland. From several quarters, the move was seen as a defection. Expecting a cursory reply concerning an event that had taken place when he was a young man, I asked my correspondent for his opinion on Heaney's migration to the Republic. He replied at length, however, in a letter bearing the brusque, black stamp of the prison center:

> The point you raised about artists and their responsibility is interesting. I have heard some of the criticism levelled at Seamus Heaney about leaving the North, and I cannot be too sure that I don't agree with it. It strikes me that if artists are to be true to themselves, then their work must in some way reflect the society they live in. If it so happens that there is a conflict in that society the artists are not absolved from portraying that conflict in their work. The problem then becomes how does this portrayal take form? Does it involve artists taking some sort of "objective" stance? I don't think that this is possible nor even

desirable. I believe that if artists live in a particular society, the conflict affects them in one way or another, and I don't believe that artists can help taking sides. Their work should in some way reflect the side they have chosen.

To many American readers, it will seem extraordinary that my correspondent had heard of the arguments marshaled against Heaney's decision to leave the North, particularly when the departure was well over a decade old. And perhaps it will seem even more extraordinary that a young man would hold such unflinchingly reasoned opinions concerning the artist's relation to society. But these firm alignments are typical of many readers and critics in Northern Ireland, and with a sophistication and urbanity rarely encountered by the American reader who faces "political" verse, these alignments appear throughout Heaney's work as one of its major structural elements. My purpose in this study has been to show how Heaney's verse has responded to the complex alignments of his homeland by renovating the authoritative techniques of pastoral literature, a literature that has traditionally entailed political resistance.

During the 1960s, Heaney became actively involved in the Catholic civil rights movement in Northern Ireland, and he regularly wrote polemical essays, still uncollected, for various publications. Before deciding in 1972 to leave Northern Ireland, he had lived in Belfast since 1957, and his residency there spanned fifteen years of social upheaval and violence: "I am fatigued," Heaney wrote in 1971 in a short Christmas piece for *The Listener,* "by a continuous adjudication between agony and injustice, swung at one moment by the long tail of race and resentment, at another by the more acceptable feelings of pity and terror."[1] Several years later in the final poem of *North* (1975), Heaney would describe himself ensconced in Wicklow as a Gaelic outlaw "escaped from the massacre," one who bides his time and weighs his "responsible *tristia.*" Exiled by Augustus to the forbidding shores of the Black Sea, Ovid composed his own *Tristia,* a poem of five books, but Ovid preferred to plead in those poems with an intractable emperor, and the poetry often suffers from the heavy-handed tactics that his preference encouraged. If Heaney's exile is self-imposed, his emperor is named Northern Ireland, and the inflammatory issues that have dominated the country's recent history reside with an imperial power in the wellsprings of Heaney's imagination.

The reader who equates political poetry with polemical versification rightly insists on discussing Heaney's work by avoiding the label "political," but the equation inaccurately restricts the term to an insignificant domain of literary endeavor. In his tactically brilliant introduction to *The Faber Book of Political Verse* (1986), Tom Paulin admits that "although the imagination can be strengthened rather than distorted by an ideology, my definition of a political poem does not assume that such poems necessarily make an ideological statement. They can instead embody a general historical awareness . . . rather than offering a specific attitude to state affairs."[2] "State affairs" in Northern Ireland have forced the Catholic population to envision themselves paradoxically as a community of exiles living at home, and such a vision accounts for much of the alienation, silence, and fear encountered in Heaney's early work. The domestic exile, robbed of the active satisfactions that attend the roving expatriate, often substitutes a defensive apathy for a concerned criticism, but Heaney has consistently avoided this position. Although one of his most characteristic and occasionally confusing postures is that of the national alien, his poetry finds its cultural stability in the development of the historical awareness that Paulin sees as comprising the vast territories of political poetry. To chart Heaney's definition and portrayal of the rural Catholic community in Northern Ireland is to understand the essentially political tenor of his verse, and to provide such an understanding is the signal burden of this study.

Perhaps "rural" is the watchword here because it leads directly to pastoral writing, the provenance of that exotic combination of country affairs and literary art. The typical reader of the early seventeenth century would not have needed Milton's epigraph to "Lycidas" to understand that the "corrupted clergy then in their height" had been taken to task by the young and zealous poet. Since Johnson's acerbic attack on "Lycidas," pastoral poetry has occupied a position of distinguished infamy, but its scintillating strategy of bringing a highly developed literary art to the chaotic arena of contemporary culture informs much of Heaney's best verse. But it informs unobtrusively—Heaney's accomplishment lies in his extension of the tradition beyond its Johnsonian and moribund domain. Readers of his verse must continually remind themselves that Heaney, perhaps more so than most other contemporary poets, is a deeply literary poet, one whose consolations often lie in the invigorating strains of the poetic tradition itself. The first chapter, then, attempts to locate, and on occasion reinterpret, the rich history of pastoral literature that provides the nurturing background for his work.

From his early days as a civil rights activist, Heaney has been acutely aware of the demanding relation, particularly in Northern Ireland, between the literary life and the political, or engaged life. Throughout his career he has pondered this difficult relationship, and it often provides him with his subject matter, particularly in the poems written after he left Belfast. Delivered as one of the T. S. Eliot Memorial Lectures at the University of Kent in 1986, Heaney's assessment of Sylvia Plath's development posed the question that has haunted him throughout his own career: "To what extent should the tongue's hedonism and frolic be in the control of the noble rider of socially responsible intellect, ethics or morals?" The allusion to Wallace Stevens's essay "The Noble Rider and the Sound of Words" clears the way for the tempered aestheticism of his own answer: "I do not in fact see how poetry can survive as a category of human consciousness if it does not put poetic considerations first—expressive considerations, that is, based upon its own genetic laws which spring into operation at the moment of lyric conception. Yet it is possible to feel all this and still concede the justice of Czeslaw Milosz's rebuke to the autocracy of such romantic presumption."[3] Heaney ultimately sides here with the moment of "lyric conception" untarnished by the "noble rider of socially responsible intellect," but his decision, as his recognition of Milosz's criticism indicates, is an equivocal one. Pastoral writing, with its dual emphasis on lyricism and social responsibility, provides for Heaney both inspiration and influence, and to keep my study within manageable limits, I have exercised various discriminations. I have avoided the temptation, for example, to include a treatment of those literary influences that did not seem strictly relevant to the pastoral mode. And even with this qualification in mind, I have omitted the work of Robert Frost because the historical awarenesses of the poets seemed in important ways to have little in common—their pastorals are conceived to accomplish radically different goals.

The one exception has been the work of John Clare, a poet whom Heaney has praised lavishly and whose work represents one of the most important and unacknowledged developments in the history of pastoral literature. Clare's poems, while insisting on their authentic portrayals of country life and language, still preserve the note of pastoral celebration that distinguished the literature before the sobrieties of the antipastoral sensibility descended on the tradition. Inheriting this blend of authenticity and celebration, Heaney establishes a voice of stern resistance sounded both in the realistic portrayals of his region and the distinctive inflections of his pentameter line. Chapter 2, then, investigates the relation between Clare and Heaney, pointing out similarities both in theme and poetic form. Because the pastoral perspectives of both poets ultimately involve political commitments, the chapter concludes with a brief discussion of political literature, a subject that naturally concerns all poets who attempt to write against the grain of the English literary hierarchy.

Yet the hierarchy of literary history, however defined, ultimately expels the fraud, the pretender, and the uninspired derivation. If Heaney's version of pastoral did not extend the tradition and force us—the idea here is Eliot's—to recognize the changes wrought on the entire order, the hierarchy would be similarly unkind to his work. *North*, Heaney's fourth collection, represents for many critics one of the major poetic accomplishments of the decade and a watershed for Heaney's own career. Published three years after the poet left Northern Ireland, it wrestles valiantly and explicitly with history, mythology, regionalism and prosody, all of which are seamlessly intertwined throughout the poems. Heaney is establishing traditions here, and his discovery of the bogs in Denmark—through a book on the subject, with graphic pictures of the preserved Iron Age bodies—provided the imaginative breakthrough that he needed to find the "images adequate," as he has phrased it, to the continual violence that afflicts Northern Ireland. The ritual sacrifices practiced by the Iron Age culture that originally settled Ireland offers the bleak precedent, and as his poems look back to that time, seeking sustenance in simple understanding, they reenact ironically a version of pastoral nostalgia. The third chapter traces this reenactment, demonstrating how the various poems of the collection develop Heaney's thorough renovations.

Renovation is tiring, exacting work, but among its many values is the renewed sense of appreciation for the original form, the original spirit. In his latest work, Heaney has abandoned the dire genealogies and the harsh intonations of *North,* and his voice seems less forbidding and more fecund than it once was. This is partly due to the resurfacing of his pentameter line, largely abandoned in *North,* and the evidence in the new poetry suggests that he is aware of the possible political defections that his new line might entail. In pastoral verse, however, a conservative prosody that tells a radical tale avoids the shrillness of testimonial writing, and in the fourth chapter I have analyzed the ways in which Heaney's verse continues to enact fundamental patterns of resistance. Even though *Field Work* (1979) and *Station Island* (1984) return to a more traditional pastoralism, particularly in the sequence from *Field Work* entitled "Glanmore Sonnets," their traditional tropes conceal a disquieting perspective that depends for its effect on the sudden realization that the pastoral world, the imaginatively perfected world of County Wicklow or rural Northern Ireland, is a world continually subject to violation and invasion. This is a more conventional strategy than that developed in *Wintering Out* (1972) and *North,* but the energies denied to formal innovation here are lustily spent in a casual eloquence that seems capable of endless incorporation.

Although the bold pastorals that surfaced in his previous collections no longer impose as they once did, their elegant and unobtrusive appearances retain the essential note of resistance that characterizes both his own verse and the various pastoral perspectives that he deftly reinvigorates. Heaney's work, born of the struggles that define his county, is regularly discussed as if it were a collection of position papers delivered to adjudicate between the claims of his art and the demands of his community. His most intimate litigations on this matter have often provided him, however, with the subject matter of his verse, and what endures in his writing is the comprehensive portrayal of the difficulties that such litigations involve. "Art's opposition to the real world," Theodor Adorno has argued, "is in the realm of form,"[4] and this is a lesson that Heaney has taken to heart. His development of the pastoral, issuing from the real world of Northern Ireland and County Wicklow, garners a portion of its authority from its canny management of the realm of form, a realm where cultural presumption and ideology are difficult to evaluate. But these evaluations, made at every level of sophistication from the grossly reductive to the overly complex, have always accompanied and occasionally dominated the reception of Irish literature since the eighteenth century, and Heaney's avowed interest in this continual dialogue is, from the Irish perspective, a traditional one.

Because Heaney was born in 1939, the year of W. B. Yeats's death, the two careers have often been unfairly aligned, but no one, particularly those who would attempt an assessment of Heaney's career to date, ignores with impunity the fact that at Heaney's current age, Yeats still had not written the bulk of poems that would establish his reputation. Mindful then of the ominous dangers that attend a book-length study of this author, I have been concerned to elucidate one of the ways in which Heaney's poetry charts its course between what has historically been described as the conflicting demands of art and politics. That conflict in the late twentieth century seems naively drawn, and Heaney's verse, in one sense, explores the nature and implications of this naiveté. The pastoral perspective that Heaney renovates is essentially an accommodating one, and this is one of the definitive characteristics of the genre—it wields the language of moral imperative that often accompanies the political voice while it nurtures the expressive intensity that dominates the register of the more private lyric. Heaney's poetry, while it remains sensitive to his country's abiding public demands, a pastoral concern, cultivates simultaneously the lyrical freedom that renders such demands palatable, and this, whether found in Virgil or Heaney, is a pastoral obsession.

Only in literary studies is it a joy to acknowledge the unceasing accumulation of debt. Irvin Ehrenpreis, who died in July 1985, presided over the early stages of this project, and the extraordinary energy with which he brought historical scholarship to bear on contemporary writing provided the definitive but unattainable example. Daniel Albright's tutelage, insisting on the accuracy of evidential argument and the nuance of the reasoned impression, helped me to resolve further the methodological quandries that confront those who would attempt a sustained study of a living writer, and without his beneficient attention, I could have more easily denied responsibility for the book's weaknesses—with his attention, my excuses wither. Dave Smith also read the manuscript, and the ideas that he propounded, directed toward broadening my sense of Heaney's place in contemporary writing, arrived in the final stages when revision is necessary and difficult. Perhaps the most ferociously logical reader that a critic might envision, Steve Cushman thinned much of the verbiage that attends the unfocused argument. And if conversations are among the fine things that need much laboring, then Tom Paulin most nobly bears Adam's curse.

I would like also to thank the English department at the University of Virginia where I received a grant that both generously allowed and quietly encouraged the completion of the project. At the University of Arkansas, Kenneth Kinnamon shielded me from many of the requirements and distractions that often attend the assistant professor, and I am deeply grateful for his benevolent lack of attention.

And finally, if tragedy, as Aristotle allowed, involves an error of judgment, or a lack of knowledge, then the principal tragedy accompanying this attempt at acknowledgment is that Cecil Lang and his wife, Violette, will never accurately judge or clearly know the extent of their influence. Altogether fitting then is my conviction that a plainly declared devotion to them will have to do.

Fayetteville, 1989

Acknowledgments

The following are reprinted by permission of Farrar, Straus and Giroux, Inc.:

"Death of a Naturalist," "At a Potato Digging," "The Early Purges," "Digging," "Twice Shy," "Follower," "Personal Helicon," "Churning Day," "The Outlaw," "The Salmon Fisher to the Salmon," "A Lough Neagh Sequence, VII" "Relic of Memory," "Shoreline," "Bann Clay," "Bog Land," "Anahorish," "Traditions," "Fodder," "The Wool Trade," "Gifts of Rain," "Toome," "Midnight," "The Tollund Man," "Summer Home," "A Winter's Tale," "Shore Woman," "Navvy," "May," "Bye Child," "The Tollund Man," "Ocean's Love to Ireland," "Antaeus," "Hercules and Antaeus," "Bog Queen," "The Grauballe Man," "North," "Belderg," "The Unacknowledged Legislator's Dream," "Singing School, 2, 6," from POEMS 1965–1975 by Seamus Heaney. Copyright © 1966, 1969, 1972, 1975, 1980 by Seamus Heaney.

"Triptych, I," "The Strand at Lough Beg," "High Summer," "The Toome Road," "September Song," "The Harvest Bow," "Glanmore Sonnets I, III, IV, VIII, IX, X" from *Field Work* by Seamus Heaney. Copyright © 1976, 1979 by Seamus Heaney.

"Making Strange," "Shelf Life," "Iron Spike," "Last Look," "The Birthplace," "The Loaning," "Changes," "Station Island V, VIII, IX" from *Station Island* by Seamus Heaney. Copyright © 1985 by Seamus Heaney.

Heaney and the Pastoral Persuasion

Abducted by Hades and spirited away to the underworld, Persephone ate several seeds from a pomegranate, the fruit traditionally associated with marriage and fertility cults. The price of her impudence was her freedom. Ingestion of the fruit sealed the marital alliance, and Demeter, Persephone's mother and one of the oldest, most powerful goddesses of the Greek pantheon, lost her daughter to an infernal son-in-law. With Zeus as her advocate, however, Demeter struck a deal with Hades, and Persephone was allowed to live with her mother for the better part of each year. During this time, the crops flourished. But when Persephone returned to the underworld to spend the remaining months with her husband, the earth became cold and barren. For the Greeks, the seasonal cycle—the pastoral calendar—sprang from a pomegranate seed.

The etymological history of the word "pomegranate" claims an essentially pastoral lineage, one that exemplifies what Puttenham, in *The Arte of English Poesie* (1589), described as the genre's tendency to employ "rude speeches to insinuate and glance at greater matters." Its Latin root "granatus" means, simply, "having many seeds," and the Romans used the substantive "granatum" to denote the same fruit, centuries before them, that the Babylonians had thrown on the floor of the bridal chamber—the fat, ripe pomegranates would burst open, scattering their seeds and, it was hoped, their fertility, on the newly married couple. Later, the French realized that the pomegranate exploded in much the same fashion as one of their own implements of war, and their coinage eventually yielded our "grenade," or "hand grenade," as it is most commonly known. This duplicity of the word "grenade," with its obvious allegiance to the martial tradition but with its informing vision of marital fertility, makes it one of the luminous words in the title poem of Heaney's first book, *Death of a Naturalist* (1966):

> Then one hot day when fields were rank
> With cowdung in the grass the angry frogs
> Invaded the flax-dam; I ducked through hedges
> To a coarse croaking that I had not heard
> Before. The air was thick with a bass chorus.
> Right down the dam gross-bellied frogs were cocked
> On sods; their loose necks pulsed like snails. Some hopped:
> The slap and plop were obscene threats. Some sat
> Poised like mud grenades, their blunt heads farting.
> I sickened, turned, and ran. The great slime kings
> Were gathered there for vengeance and I knew
> That if I dipped my hand the spawn would clutch it.[1]

Puttenham would not have acknowledged "Death of a Naturalist" as a work of pastoral art, even though its language is muscularly rude. The glittering pastures that he envisaged lay far from the open countryside, and these "self-same hills," when depicted in "Lycidas" and early Renaissance poetry, arrive with cartographic accuracy from Virgil's "Eclogue 4," an eclogue radiant with the promise of a restored Golden Age. Such promises, however, make exacting demands on the poet. To dream of a Golden Age, to create the illusion of perfection, pastoral writers sparingly deployed the particularizing detail that might suddenly have transported their readers from an Arcadian vale to an English valley. A decision to write pastoral poetry automatically entailed formal requirements, and these forms dictated the predictable conformations of pastoral landscapes. Suited in such constrictive armor, the genre would seem impervious to the obsessive particularity of Heaney's poem. But even the earliest English pastorals are partly shorn of their Grecian garb, incorporating specific details of the English countryside while preserving themes and ideas inherited from the classical models. Digression often breeds irrelevancy, but the various registers of the pastoral voice are nowadays as elusive as they once were alluring; Heaney's version of pastoral develops several strategies native to the tradition, and an analysis of these strategies will provide the historical background necessary to assess the exact nature of Heaney's accomplishment.

With its opening invitation, Robert Herrick's "The Wake" (1648) recalls an invitation found in Christopher Marlowe's "The Passionate Shepherd to His Love" (1599), written a half-century earlier. "Come live with me, and be my love," began Marlowe's shepherd, in the land with "Vallies, groves, hills and fields" that have become for many readers the emblematic topography of classical pastoral. But Herrick's speaker, perhaps equally idealistic in his travel plans, exhibits a more English, more localized sense of place than that of his predecessor:

> Come, Anthea, let us two
> Go to Feast, as others do.
> Tarts and Custards, Creams and Cakes,
> Are the Junketts still at Wakes:
> Unto which the Tribes resort,
> Where the business is the sport.
> Morris-dancers thou shalt see,
> Marian, too, in Pagentrie:
> And a Mimick to devise
> Many grinning properties.
> Players there will be, and those
> Base in action as in clothes;
> Yet with strutting they will please
> The incurious Villages.
> Near the dying of the day
> There will be a *Cudgell*-Play
> Where a *Coxcomb* will be broke,
> Ere a good *word* can be spoke:
> But the anger ends all here,
> Drenched in Ale or drowned in Beere.
> Happy Rusticks, best content
> With the cheapest Merriment;
> And possesse no other feare
> Than to want the Wake next Yeare.

The vision here of rural simplicity and abundance is common to pastoral writing from its beginnings in Theocritus and Virgil. If Herrick's seems a somewhat decadent, condescending version—his rustics, after all, are "drowned in Beere"—his affable setting, a Bruegel scene in all its

3

particularity, begins to color the pastoral horizon. In 1629, Herrick became a country clergyman in Devonshire; since 1623, he had been a member of Jonson's literary coterie in London, and the splenetic rural clergyman never forgot the splendid royal courtier. Although employing the generalized, pastoral themes of simplicity and abundance, the poem relies on its subversive particularity—as the tarts and custards yield to ale, beer, and drunkenness—to chart the poet's disgruntlement.

With one eye on the shepherd and the other, for example, on Milton's "Corrupted clergy," pastoral poets have always been walleyed, and this skewed vision accounts for the pastoral's notoriety as a genre susceptible to social and political commentary. In Heaney's case, the concreteness and vivid detail of his writing subsume the several pastoral conventions that still survive to structure his poems. At first glance, his work has little in common with what is habitually labeled pastoral. If "Death of a Naturalist," a poem whose "fields were rank with cow-dung," appears perfectly opposed to the "beds of roses" in Marlowe's "The Passionate Shepherd to His Love," such opposing appearances are resolved by Puttenham's suggestion that pastorals employ their rude diction to "insinuate and glance at greater matters." Where grenades are found in Heaney's work, so too are pomegranates, and this subliminal attempt to reconcile the violent particularity of his landscape with some of the generalizing conventions of pastoral poetry aligns him with an important aspect of the genre's tradition.

Displaying these powers of insinuation that Puttenham described, much of Heaney's work remains faithful to its pastoral origins. To speak of contemporary poetry as pastoral in nature is not to speak of its adherence to a set of formal conventions. Swinburne's elegy, "Ave Atque Vale," which appeared in 1868, claims the honor of being the last unquestionably great English elegy to boast of its classical parentage, and by then even that magnificent lamentation seems a step removed from late Victorian verse—the poem excels as much in its nostalgic rarity as in its stunning poetic accomplishments. Heaney would have bewildered Puttenham, as Swinburne would have dismayed him, but he would also have been brought up short by the antipastoral, by Stephen Duck's "The Thresher's Labour" (1736). Although originally from the Wiltshire countryside, he was eventually adopted as a kind of court poet in London, and as a consequence, his verse lost much of its idiosyncratic stamp. Yet Duck's best work insists on the vigorously revisionary impulse that characterizes antipastoral writing and survives to build the foundation for the dissenting voice, the voice of the Northern Irish

Catholic heard in Heaney's verse. Here is Duck, in "The Thresher's Labour," protesting and disabusing:

> The Shepherd well may tune his Voice to sing
> Inspir'd with all the Beauties of the Spring.
> No fountains murmur here, no Lambkins play,
> No Linnets warble, and no Fields look gay;
> 'Tis all a gloomy, melancholy Scene,
> Fit only to provoke the Muse's Spleen.

But even older, less drastic examples show a similar sensibility. Would Puttenham have recognized the pastures surrounding Penshurst in Jonson's poem of 1616, a time much closer to his own? Though he would have found satyrs lurking and muses lounging and dryads gamboling about the grounds, Puttenham would also have heard a wistful appraisal of feudal harmony at the Penshurst manor, a house whose walls were "rear'd with no man's ruine, no man's grone. . . ." The manor house, once a symbol of power and patronage, of a cooperative understanding between lord and laborer, already appears in the poem bathed in the flattering glow of a distant Golden Age. Because the social order of rural seventeenth-century England relied upon the stabilizing influence and regional authority of the major families, James I had tried to force the English nobility to forsake the indulgent pleasures of London and assume their rightful post as lord and lady of the manor house. Jonson's poem, celebrating Penshurst, the ancestral home of Sidney, presents an enticing vision of Protestant moderation ("Thou art not, Penshurst, built to envious show") and English ascendancy ("Sidney's copse").

But even in the early seventeenth century, some poets were hearing the laborer's groan; some were beginning to claim the hardships of the laborer's life as a subject for poetry and were doing so by deploying their disgruntlements as correctives to pastoral commonplaces. A new realism is afoot, and the first two couplets of Francis Quarles's "On the Plough-Man" (1635) succinctly contrasts the traditional pastoral image with the author's qualifying observation, at once generic and political in its objection:

> I heare the whistling *Plough-man,* all day long,
> Sweetning his labour with a chearefull song:
> His Bed's a Pad of *Straw;* His dyet course;
> In both, he fares not better then his *Horse.* . . .

As startled as Puttenham would have been to find these poems included in a discussion of pastoral poetry, he would have sympathized in equal measure with the involved arguments that landed them there. Quarles's objection represents an early example of the pastoral's propensity for social and political criticism. Part of Heaney's success in dramatizing the various quandaries faced by the Catholic population of rural Northern Ireland derives from the pastoral's ability to undermine a literary convention with a particularized description. The toppled assumption—whether political or literary—is a less visible result of pastoral writing than of polemical speech making, but the tradition has provided verbal strategies that allow Heaney to depict his own culture in ways that reveal its integrity while gently dispersing the English culture that would disfranchise him. The neat distinctions implied by the terms "pastoral" and "antipastoral" seem to clarify the essential development of a long tradition in English writing: by the late eighteenth and early nineteenth centuries, the laborer's groan was at least as loud as the shepherd's song, and the literature that had once celebrated the harmonies of the countryside now exposed the poverty and hardships suffered by its people.

Yet the story is not so simple. When read closely, the early commentaries reveal a clear awareness of the difference between a plowed field edged in hawthorne and an emerald pasture rimmed in laurel. Real shepherds, the commentators have always claimed, never enjoyed the carefree ease of the rural life depicted by the classical pastoral. One of the first attempts to develop a systematic exposition of the rudiments and origins of English verse, Puttenham's treatise devotes little space to the pastoral mode or "kind." But his reply to the widely popular notion that the pastoral, because it dealt with an ancient, even prehistoric way of life, represented the oldest form of writing in existence shows that he understood the essential problems confronting all critics who attempt to define the literature:

> Some be of the opinion . . . that the pastoral Poesie . . . should be the
> first of any other . . . because, they say, the shepheards and haywards
> assemblies and meetings when they kept their cattell and heards in the
> common fields and forests was the first familiar conversation, and their
> babble and talk under bushes and shadie trees, the first disputation and
> contentious reasoning. . . . And all this may be true, for before there
> was a shepheard keeper of his owne, or of some other bodies flocke,
> there was none owner in the world, quick cattell being the first property

of any forreine possession. . . . But for all this, I do deny that the *Eglogue* should be the first and most ancient forme of artificiall Poesie, being perswaded that the Poet devised the *Eglogue* long after *drammatick* poems . . . to insinuate and glance at greater matters. . . .

(book I, chapter 18)

Puttenham gives full credence to the methodology of an argument that would define a literary genre by locating its origin in the world of daily affairs, of "quick cattell"; when he finally discourages the application of that argument to the "Eglogue," he does so by implying that a realistic representation of the country life was never the intention of pastoral writing. But the charge had been leveled, and an essential aspect of the pastoral had been recognized: in its attempt to describe the perfected rural society, a society removed from the daily affairs of the city and capable of rendering implicit judgments on those affairs, the best pastoral writing developed rhetorical strategies both to describe the world as it is and to envisage the world as it had been in a past Golden Age. Heaney's earliest verse often depicts the fondest recollections of a childhood passed in the country with an aggressive, even militaristic diction, emphasizing at once the integrity of his culture and the violence that has become a part of its daily ritual. Puttenham is fully aware of the pastoral's natural proclivity for commenting on social or political affairs, for glancing at "greater matters," and he soundly rebuffs the theory that the literature represents the original literary endeavors of the rural society it described.

Puttenham discouraged such notions of authenticity but recognized at the same time that the pastoral's ability to keep one eye trained on the realistic, particularized landscape and one on the idealized vista of a better world represented the genre's most compelling feature. He does not banish the English and European disciples of Virgil to a charmed pleasance; he argues that the countryside, with all of its trappings and accouterments, provides the writer with a vehicle for glancing at matters beyond its immediate purview. Puttenham's elaborate refutations were designed precisely to emphasize the artifice of the genre, to prevent the sixteenth-century reader from viewing the pastoral as a piece of sociological field work. By the eighteenth century, pastoral poets had become so dependent on this same literary artifice only hinted at by Puttenham that critics were once again correcting abuses. When shepherds debate foreign policy, they argued, readers are asked to suspend their disbelief beyond credibility.

7

The idea of credibility, in one guise or another, has informed both the major critiques and the persuasive examples of pastoral literature from Puttenham's time to the present. One luminous example chosen from the imposing body of critical material demonstrates how thoroughgoing was this corrosive worry over the shepherd's life in the hills and the accuracy of its representation in the work of art. The sophistication of an articulate shepherd has historically been one of the least tolerated sophistications in English writing, and Dr. Johnson's diatribe on "Lycidas," that "easy, vulgar" poem, is one of the most infamous attacks in the critical canon. Continually, the pastoral has confronted the accusations of debunking realists, and the confrontation emphasizes the curiously large degree of social responsibility and realism—the literary device most often associated with social responsibility—expected of the pastoral author. Johnson, though not one of the early commentators, neatly and caustically speaks for the many doubters who preceded him:

> It is therefore improper to give the title of a pastoral to verses in which the speakers, after the slight mention of their flocks, fall to complaints of errors in the church and corruptions in the government, or to lamentations of the death of some illustrious person, whom when once the poet has called a shepherd, he has no longer any labour upon his hands, but can make the clouds weep, and lilies wither, and the sheep hang their heads, without art or learning, genius, or study.[2]

Nothing is so tiringly conventional as an insignificant pastoral, and even those writers most invigorated by its formal strictures seem wary of the living shepherd who wearily follows his sheep from grazing to grazing. The eighteenth century, remarkable in this context because it was the last era to view the composition of the pastoral as an ordinary poetic enterprise, abounds with theoretical writing on the subject. Pope, for example, cared nothing for tooth and claw, and his comments on the pastoral portray a writer aware of the fact that shepherds named Corydon, wandering through an anglicized Arcadia, do not face the hardships of shepherds named Michael who move stones at Grasmere. That Pope would even respond to such an obvious assertion emphasizes how enduring this concern for authenticity and credibility had become for both critics and poets alike. In his "Discourse on Pastoral Poetry," he states baldly that the work of the pastoral poet lies "in exposing the best side only of a shepherd's life, and in concealing its miseries."[3] Although not all early pastoral writers had been so idealistic—not Spenser, for example, in "January," from *The Shepheardes Calender*—Pope's position represents the purest excrescence of pastoral theory, emphasizing its power to idealize but ignoring its tendency to recognize the quotidian reality and its attendant miseries.

Extremity in religion and literature breeds heresy, and when Pope claimed that two and only two of Virgil's *Eclogues* were truly pastoral works, he showed how exhausted traditions end in denial. Although Johnson, on the other hand, does not suggest that the poet dwell on miseries, he clearly presses for a measure of credibility. This represents a significant shift in emphasis. By attacking several glamorous abuses of pastoral writing, he makes us suspicious of it all. Johnson's strictures, unlike Pope's, are less definitive and more hopeful.

Johnson's witty assessment was prompted by his own famous definition of pastoral earlier in the same piece: a "representation of an action or passion by its effects upon a country life." These actions or passions, then, must not be "inconsistent with a country life." It is difficult—and unfair—to guess how Puttenham would have replied to Johnson; the body of material that concerned Puttenham was smaller and more orderly in spirit than the vast and varied pastorals that Johnson read. As the ranks of the literature swelled, encompassing the lyric, the elegy, the romance, and the drama, so too did the definitions. Whereas the critics of Puttenham's time could quibble over the details of a convention, Johnson's age was attempting to reconcile the inconsistencies of a literary behemoth that had begun to violate, transgress, and redefine its traditional boundaries.

Both Puttenham and Johnson were bothered by the issue of credibility, and to justify their anxiety they discovered a reason for it: the language of pastoral was not the authentic language of the pasture. Literary realism, in nineteenth-century fiction, was most often summoned to correct abuses and reveal hardships, and the pastoral did not escape untainted by this important development. The reformative zeal for authenticity, when it finally evolved as the domineering concern of the poetry, helped to form the characteristic tone of the antipastoral, a relatively modern development of the late eighteenth and early nineteenth centuries. Crabbe's *The Village* (1783), for example, intends to indict social injustice by providing "the real picture of the poor. . . ." But this is a literary revolution in its late stages. The beginnings of a healthy skepticism, the first stirrings of a countermovement against the established conventions of pastoral writing, were evident as early as the sixteenth century. From the beginning, the literature developed tactics of diversion and inference that characterize Heaney's development as he consolidates his savvy political voice.

The earliest pastoralists obviously had not seen the stern reprimands handed down by Johnson. Spenser, identified by Puttenham as "that other Gentleman who wrote the late shepheardes Callender," was well aware of the satirical possibilities inherent in one of the most prevalent pastoral conventions, the poet, or in Spenser's version, the knight as shepherd. In book 6, canto 9 of *The Faerie Queene*, Sir Calidore has arrived in Arcadia and fallen in love with Pastorella; when she proves invulnerable to his knightly charms, he changes his "loftie looke" for the authentic look, the "shepheards weed," and quickly wins her love. Lest this seem too blatantly erotic, the story takes yet another turn. What Pastorella had loved in her lowly shepherd was, in fact, his courteous qualities, shining through the warp and woof of his native flannel. Eventually, blood as well as water seeks its own level: Pastorella was of a pedigree higher than had previously been suspected, so their attraction to each other, in both the environmental and hereditary sense, was a natural one.

The masquerade reveals a more serious aspect of pastoral, one in which Calidore assumes the appearance of a shepherd, traditionally connoting honesty, even gullibility, to further his designs on Pastorella. When Calidore strikes out across the fields with Pastorella on his arm, he is using the pastoral mode literally, in Puttenham's terms, to "insinuate and glance" at other women, and the reader witnesses a convincing demonstration of the pastoral's capacity for deception and subterfuge. Today Irish nationalists dressed in English tweeds roam the streets of London, occasionally lionized by the literary community they oppose, so artful has been their opposition. In 1983, Heaney published a response to his inclusion in an anthology of verse entitled *The Penguin Book of Contemporary British Poetry;* his rural and "anxious" muse is "roused on her bed among the furze," and his abdication reveals how successful his ruse has been:

> Yet doubts, admittedly, arise
> When somebody who publishes
> In LRB and TLS,
> > *The Listener—*
> In other words, whose audience is,
> > Via Faber,

> A British one, is characterized
> As British. But don't be surprised
> If I demur, for, be advised
>   My passport's green.
> No glass of ours was ever raised
>   To toast *The Queen*.[4]

This inclination toward subterfuge, which is in turn facilitated by the genre's tendency to cast its characters in deceptively conventional roles, is clearest in Spenser's "Colin Clouts Come Home Again." The poem is organized as a dialogue between Colin Clout, who has just returned from a trip across the sea, and ten shepherds and shepherdesses, who ply him with questions about his traveling partner, his sea voyage, and his visit to the court of Cynthia. The poem details an Irish homecoming, and although Colin's sympathies are not those of a modern Irish nationalist, the poem remains a skillful pastoral rendition of the various skepticisms that historically characterized relations between Ireland and England. Spenser's biography has figured prominently in many interpretations of the work, and commentators have closely examined the various landscapes of the poem, particularly the one portrayed in the myth of Bregog and Mulla (ll.104–55). The precise situation of the rivers, the mountain called "Mole . . ./That walls the Northside of Armulla Dale," and "the ragged ruines"—all of these specific geographical details have led critics to believe that the home referred to in the title is indeed Spenser's Cork County estate. And near the end of the poem, when Colin has described the bounties of Cynthia's court, Thestylis wonders why anyone would return from such a happy place "to this barrein soyle/Where cold and care and penury do dwell" (ll.656–57). Colin's answer begins the section on the corruption of the court.

Thestylis's dreary depiction of his homeland has led some critics to speculate on Spenser's happiness in Ireland: perhaps these descriptions represent affective portraits of Spenser's thoughts and feelings while living away from England. But the evaluation of the poem is not solely a matter of biography. Spenser's descriptions, most fruitfully read in the tradition of the perfected landscape, the earthly Eden, incorporate varying levels of particularity and biographical reference within familiar pastoral contexts. Several shepherds, more obviously than others, represent important historical figures; some rivulets more clearly than others portray actual streams.

But the idealized landscapes in Spenser's pastoral poems often show traces of the persistent attention to regional detail that will dominate late twentieth-century poetry. Under the aegis of the pastoral, much of this poetry finds its distant and surprising ancestor. In Heaney's work this persistence in meticulous description is carefully marshaled to transcend its particularity, creating that distinctly pastoral tension between the idealized landscape of the past—the Golden Age—and the realistic depiction of Irish geography. In a poem such as "Anahorish," Heaney imagines that the name itself possesses ineffable powers of cultural sovereignty. Irish place-names in the United Kingdom become for Heaney subversive incantations that both glorify his Celtic lineage and establish its integrity in British Northern Ireland. The poem dexterously appropriates a landscape politically British in its legal demarcation but linguistically Irish in its nomenclature:

> My "place of clear water,"
> the first hill in the world
> where springs washed into
> the shiny grass
>
> and darkened cobbles
> in the bed of the lane.
> *Anahorish*, soft gradient
> of consonant, vowel-meadow,
>
> after-image of lamps
> swung through the yards
> on winter evenings.
> With pails and barrows
>
> those mound-dwellers
> go waist-deep in mist
> to break the light ice
> at wells and dunghills.

The genealogy established here between the people of Heaney's childhood and the "mound dwellers"—they are practically coalesced into one ancestor—lies entrenched beyond the reach of English bloodlines, and the poem combines a quiet celebration of an Irish childhood with a strenuous resistance to cultural hegemony. Within the pastoral context, these often contrary concerns are reconciled.

The allegorical quality of pastoral writing has been a stable part of the tradition since Virgil's time. But the literature carefully discriminates between these conventional references to living people and the broader, less conventional attempt to incorporate into the poetry the specific details of character or landscape that might dissipate the gleaming innocence of the pastoral vision. Accordingly, the matter of poetic diction, whether based on the regional pidgin or the royal parlance, became an important issue in pastoral theory. In *The Renewal of Literature*, Richard Poirier argues that the "self-analytical mode" of the modernist text instituted a "form of cultural skepticism," which in varying degrees "is to be found earlier on, as in, say, Spenser's transformations of the allegorical tradition. . . ."[5] Following a rapturous description of Cynthia in "Colin Clout Comes Home Again," Cuddy chides Colin for his elevated speech:

> *Colin* (said *Cuddy* then) thou has forgot
> Thy selfe, me seemes, too much, to mount so hie:
> Such loftie flight, base shepheard seemeth not,
> From flocks and fields, to Angel and to skie.
>
> (11.616–19)

The pastoral illusion here is qualified, if slightly so. By reminding Colin that shepherds must use a baser English than the one he has been using, Cuddy does not argue for a dialectal purity but ironically insists on one of the genre's conventions: in essence he reminds Colin of Puttenham's notion that pastoral writers must employ "rude speeches." Governed by this irony, Colin's lofty flights become the unconventional element of the passage. But this insight comes at the end of a circuitous path; the rigidity of the pastoral form has begun to loosen a little, revealing glimpses of the world beyond the pasture.

The subject of poetic diction concerns all poets, but Irish authors have addressed the matter with exceptional vigor, emphasizing the political implications of choosing or ignoring various words and figures of speech. Heaney's etymological interests have occasioned several of his finest poems, but only a few have openly addressed the political questions that confront the Irish writer. From *Wintering Out*, the first section of "Traditions" states the case succinctly:

Intro

Our guttural muse
was bulled long ago
by the alliterative tradition,
her uvula grows

vestigial, forgotten
like the coccyx
or a Brigid's Cross
yellowing in some outhouse

while custom, that "most
sovereign mistress,"
beds us down into
the British Isles.

The feeling of linguistic displacement in the poem is shared by many Irish writers. Tom Paulin, a poet and critic from Belfast who currently resides in England, has argued passionately for the establishment of an Irish English dictionary, finding an analogy in Noah Webster's dictionary and his *Dissertations,* the treatises that examined the influence of the American language on the country's concepts of nationhood. Such a dictionary in Ireland would have a redemptive effect:

> Many words which now appear simply gnarled, or which "make strange" or seem opaque to most readers, would be released into the shaped flow of a new public language. . . . A confident concept of Irish English would substantially increase the vocabulary and this would invigorate the written language. A language that lives lithely on the tongue ought to be capable of becoming the flexible written instrument of a complete cultural idea.[6]

"A new public language," "a complete cultural idea"—the phrases resonate with a shrewd and subtle republicanism. The dialectal words and rhythms in Heaney's verse, similar to the "rude speeches," those wayward words often labeled "variant" by lexicographers, represent the common inheritance of the Catholic culture of rural Northern Ireland, a culture that from Heaney's standpoint has suffered political displacement. The pastoral, freely admitting allegorical language and implicitly encouraging resistance and deception, allows Heaney to enshrine his culture while fashioning a cogent and subversive response to the problems faced by the Catholic minority in Northern Ireland.

The word "subversive," when used accurately in this context, describes the way in which pastoral writing balances social criticism and aesthetic design. Pastoral poetry had always been used for polemical purposes, and when Milton prefaces "Lycidas" with his announcement that he "by occasion foretells the ruin of our corrupted Clergy," he is working within a well-defined literary tradition of political and religious dissent. Accordingly, the American reader who innocently opens Empson's seminal work on the subject, *Some Versions of Pastoral* (1935), will be surprised to find the first chapter entitled "Proletarian Literature." Empson begins by introducing the subject of "proletarian art" and declares it "important to try and decide what the term might mean. . . ."

His diction alone plays to the political sensibility, a sensibility that will bear fruit when evaluating Heaney's version of pastoral. Aside from several notable examples, academic criticism in America has avoided political engagement, and the shopworn tenets of New Criticism, with their emphasis on poetic form and an ahistorical aesthetic, provide an excellent example. The few critics and poets who undertook the sweeping examinations such engagements required have traditionally earned the unfortunate title "men of letters." Edmund Wilson appears on this role, and, surely, T. S. Eliot.

Yet for the English and Irish critics, raised on the subterfuges of Auden's early poetry, on the volunteer spirit fostered by the Spanish Civil War, and finally on the hardships of a World War fought at home, the political dimension of literature excited a compelling, if sometimes breast-beating, urgency in many of the writers. Empson is always honing his insights into pastoral literature with the gritty observations of a social worker. Although Heaney's verse generally transcends the confinements of the political arena, the confrontations encountered there account for one of the defining strengths of his work and clarify his relation to the pastoral. Here is an example of Empson's method: "Of course there are plenty of skilled workers in England who are proud of their skill, and you can find men of middle age working on farms who say they prefer the country to the town, but anything like what I am trying to call pastoral is a shock to the Englishman who meets it on the Continent."[7] Empson's sociopolitical program always stands as the foil for his brilliance as a literary critic; the work of art, whether *Paradise Lost* or *Alice in Wonderland,* always corners his attention. But not all critics so acrobatically walk the fence between facile sloganeering and felicitous phrasing. Other problems associated with the term "pastoral" must be resolved before Heaney's work assumes its rightful place in the tradition.

15

In a review of *The Penguin Anthology of Pastoral Poetry,* Heaney summarizes his opinion regarding the modern usage of the word, and if he lacks the accuracy theoreticians might require, he nonetheless reflects a widespread opinion: " 'Pastoral' is a term that has been extended by usage until its original meaning has been largely eroded. For example, I have occasionally talked of the country-side where we live in Wicklow as being pastoral rather than rural, trying to impose notions of a beautified landscape on the word, in order to keep 'rural' for the unselfconscious face of raggle-taggle farmland."[8] In most informal writing, the word "idyllic" often substitutes for "pastoral"; a cottage in the country might reasonably be described as both "idyllic" and "pastoral" because either word conjures up a similar range of associations. Yet if Heaney seems perfectly suited to be a pastoral poet, why then does he resist—it is as if he were being sentenced—the title "idyllic poet"? The latter phrase assigns him to the charmed existence of "farmer Allan at the farm abode," as Tennyson has it in "Dora," while the former commands for him the integrity of a literary tradition. The term "pastoral," often undefined and inaccurately deployed, commands a general field of reference that seems to describe much of Heaney's early poetry. But the poet's own definition of the term limits its usage: "beautified" will simply not suffice for the frogs in "Death of a Naturalist" with their "blunt heads farting."

Certain themes and literary strategies are native to the pastoral tradition, and their recurrence, with or without the attendant shepherd, shapes the modern pastoral. Perspective, theme, and imagery are the watchwords. In the same review, Heaney continues: "Obviously, we are unlikely to find new poems about shepherds that engage us as fully as 'Lycidas,' but surely the potent dreaming of a Golden Age or the counter-cultural celebration of simpler life-styles or the nostalgic projection of the garden on childhood are still occasionally continuous with the tradition as it is presented here."[9] Heaney's point is clear. Although much of the traditional machinery of the pastoral—the shepherds, the singing contests, the personification of the natural world in its elegiac posture—fell long ago into a benign disrepair, the desires that fueled the machinery, "the potent dreaming of a Golden Age," remain immediate, vivid, and urgent. John Lynen, in his book on Robert Frost's pastoral-ism, clarifies the relation between literary convention and pastoral myth, a clarification that succinctly explicates an essential feature of the genre's development:

The conventions are not the true basis of pastoral, but an outgrowth of something deeper and more fundamental. Pastoralism requires an established myth of the rural world, and the conventions gradually developed through tradition belong to the myth of Arcadia. They are formalized symbols whose function is to evoke an imaginative vision of this world. But Arcadia is not the only version of rural life, and it is possible for a poet to write true pastorals within the context of some other mythic rural world.[10]

The work of each author will have its own unique shape, its own version of pastoral. Such freedoms encourage abuses in the literary critic who finds traces of pastoral in any poem, novel, song, or play remotely concerned with the country life. Open doors can lead to indiscrimination, and prolonged, persistent indiscrimination to fatuity and mental flatulence. Andrew Ettin, one of the most recent critics attempting to distill the essence of pastoral writing, offers this insight:

> Not all nature writing . . . is pastoral. What makes a work pastoral are its attitudes toward the natural world and human experience. In pastoral literature, experiences and emotions are contained within finite limits. Those limits are implied by the patterns revealed within the natural world and within the pastoral way of life, consonant with the patterns of the natural world. The containment is necessitated by the fragility or delicacy of the experiences and emotions, or by tension between pastoral and nonpastoral experience.[11]

Ettin shrewdly embraces what others before him have disparaged. Pastoral experience, fragile and delicate, is contained and circumscribed by nonpastoral experience, and the resulting tension between the two worlds characterizes most pastoral literature. When he uses the word "attitudes," he is tipping his hat to another critic whose helpful insights Ettin acknowledges. In his book, *Pastoral Forms and Attitudes,* Harold Toliver gives us a sound piece of advice for shaping our own attitudes toward the latter-day pastoral. Aside from analyzing the predictable authors such as Spenser, Shakespeare, Marvell, and Milton, he includes chapters on Stevens and Bellow. Of his introductory statements, one is worthy of engraving in stone: "Whether or not the texts examined here need all be considered 'pastorals' is not as important finally as our discovering something in them through this lens that would be less noticeable through another."[12] Much of Heaney's poetry is enlarged and clarified through such a lens. His enlargements and clarifications not only situate him in a literary tradition, they reevaluate the literature of that tradition, echoing, as they do, the old forgotten melodies.

Virgil's *Eclogues*, part of the old and influential melodies, collect the richest gathering of pastoral themes, conventions, and situations in the literary tradition. The essential spirit of "Lycidas" resides there as do the more liberal interpretations of the twentieth-century pastoral. And the *Eclogues* are no less helpful in providing a model of the country life politicized, a perspective that will dominate Heaney's literary strategy. In its infancy, English pastoral writing exercised a subtle skepticism concerning the integrity of the rural myth; and, more often than not, this skepticism took the form of a landscape described in assertive, particularized detail or a shepherd's formal speech punctuated occasionally by the calculated embarrassment, a diction that seemed inconsistent with the literary standards mandated by pastoral conventions. In Spenser, the asperities of that satire—along with the bleaker moments of *The Shepheardes Calender*—were tempered by the health and pleasure of life in Arcadia or Cynthia's court. Although the Book of Genesis provides the ancient precedent for viewing gardens as cradles of natural innocence, Virgil's *Eclogues* more accurately register the feelings of ambivalence and deception that became associated with the charmed life of the shepherd or farmer. In "Eclogue I," Meliboeus has been evicted from his farm, and as he drives his goats along the road he happens on Tityrus, who through various machinations has been allowed to keep his land. The dialogue that follows deftly balances the joys of the landowner with the miseries of the dispossessed. As it ends, however, Tityrus invites Meliboeus to pass the night with him:

> Hic tamen hanc mecum poteras requiescere noctem
> fronde super viridi: sunt nobis mitia poma,
> castaneae molles et pressi copia lactis;
> et iam summa procul villarum culmina fumant
> maioresque cadunt altis de montibus umbrae.[13]

> [But you could still spend the night with me;
> I've got a good bed, my apples are ripe,
> the chestnuts are just right, and there's plenty of cheese.
> And over there smoke curls from the rooftops
> as the shadows from the mountains fall down.]

The presiding beauty of the last two lines masks the brutality of the evictions and resettlements carried out after Julius Caesar was murdered in 44 B.C. Avoiding elision, the sleek dactyls of the verses—these are perhaps the two most melodious and entrancing lines in the poem—move along as crisply as dactyls can, contrasting with the somber march of the emigrants who crowd the road of exile. Ettin's concept of tension is working here at its highest pitch. And although the fluency of the lines successfully counters the dire exigencies of the emigration, Tityrus's version of pastoral seems somehow skewed and callous. Virgil's artistry is unquestionable. As the graceful accomplishment of the writing averts the reader's gaze from Meliboeus's march, the poet's voluptuous descriptions momentarily displace Meliboeus's plight, the main subject of the poem. Virgil's ruse, once uncovered, allows the reader to participate in the restoration of the truth, of nonpastoral experience. Virgil uses ironically a mellifluous and conventional language to question the order and harmony of the community depicted in his poem. And as long as Virgil has accomplished such literary subterfuges, he will not be disappointed if the principles currently structuring the redivision of the Italian countryside are questioned. Implication is the essence of strong pastoral writing, and this quality above all others distinguishes Heaney's verse.

In the hands of Pope and the neoclassicists, the pastoral often seems little more than a five-finger exercise, and this manipulative literariness concerned George Crabbe, one of the vociferous reformers of the eighteenth century. In *The Country and the City,* Raymond Williams neatly summarizes Crabbe's program and offers an effective way of looking at those two hypnotic lines that closed the "Eclogue I":

> What we can see happening . . . is the conversion of conventional pastoral into a localised dream and then, increasingly, in the late seventeenth and early eighteenth centuries, into what can be offered as a description and thence an idealisation of actual English country life and its social and economic relations. It was against this, as well as against the conventional simplicities of literary neo-pastoral, that Crabbe was making his protest.[14]

The oppressive political context in which Virgil wrote partly determined his glimmering description of the Italian countryside; but idealization, as Augustus knew, is the sinister face of flattery. The lines, though momentarily convincing with their seductive beauty, intend otherwise; they draw attention to themselves, and their spell is broken. In Virgil and, to a far greater degree, in Crabbe, the pastoral vision recognizes the recalcitrance of its conventions and even depends upon the resulting tensions. This represents one of the genre's defining characteristics.

Virgil's *Eclogues*, then, the classical provenance for much English pastoral writing, was fired in the crucible of imperial politics, and the literary strategies developed by Virgil accorded the genre an intricate language of reference and judgment. And this characteristic still distinguishes the works that would lay claim to a Virgilian heritage. American criticism of Heaney's verse has often proved helpful in uncovering its particular psychological orientations and obsessions, its formal niceties, and its expanding influence on other writers; but his varied pastorals encourage, as pastorals always have, an examination of the social and political exigencies that structure the various elements of his verse. Heaney's early poetry, with its careful description of farm life, was written during the 1960s, a time of upheaval and political turmoil in Northern Ireland. Published in 1969, *Door Into the Dark*, Heaney's second book, appeared in the same year that a group of men, unhappy with Cathal Goulding's leadership of the Irish Republican Army, founded their own Provisional Army Council, known simply as the "Provos," the violent, now infamous wing of the IRA. The organization had historically recruited its members from the lower-class farmers, but the extensive rioting that occurred in Belfast during 1969 encouraged a segment of the urban youth to enlist. American readers must constantly remind themselves of the horrific struggles that became a daily reality for the citizens of Belfast and Derry. When asked to describe his life in Belfast, Heaney remarked in 1971 that "I've found myself saying that things aren't too bad in our part of the town: a throwaway consolation meaning that we don't expect to be caught in a crossfire if we step into the street."[15]

Heaney's renditions of a childhood passed in County Derry often seem constructed from the perspective of one who has weathered the long political struggles of his community; a language of confrontation and deception pervades even the simplest rural vignettes, and this tension between the nostalgic simplicity of farm life and the disabusing complexity of political strife aligns much of the verse with the Virgilian tradition. A poem such as "The Outlaw" from *Door Into the Dark* describes how the poet, as a child, took a fertile cow to be inseminated by an unlicensed bull, an "outlaw." The mannerly concision of the couplets is constantly undercut by the foreboding sense of illegality that issues from the diction of the poem. The principals of the poem, a kind of barnyard microcosm, are united by their brief and essentially comic collusion against the agricultural laws concerning the licensing of bulls. Paulin has argued that the political poem is not one that necessarily makes an ideological statement but one that embodies "a general historical awareness," and here an essential element of rural life—the breeding of cattle—is described in terms that aptly represent the alienation experienced by the Irish Catholic in Northern Ireland.[16]

The first five couplets of the poem capture the experience of undergoing an initiation, of gaining entrance to a clandestine society united by its active resistance to an established law of the community. But the poem does not plead for political action; it embodies an awareness from the child's perspective of the essential ingredients that often accompany resistance. Secrecy, danger, profiteering, collusion—all are here:

> Kelly's kept an unlicensed bull, well away
> From the road: you risked fine but had to pay
>
> The normal fee if cows were serviced there.
> Once I dragged a nervous Friesian on a tether
>
> Down a lane of alder, shaggy with catkin,
> Down to the shed the bull was kept in.
>
> I gave Old Kelly the clammy silver, though why
> I could not guess. He grunted a curt "Go by.
>
> Get up on that gate." And from my lofty station
> I watched the business-like conception.

Through a careful compilation of several words and phrases that gradually develop the intended mood ("risked fine," "nervous," "clammy," and "business-like conception"), Heaney constructs a rural vignette as he implicates ever so slightly the foreboding world beyond the corral. Here, the delineations of that world avoid the easy labels of Irish and English or Protestant and Catholic, but the note of confrontation, essential to pastoral, sounds clearly.

From the same volume, "The Salmon Fisher to the Salmon" imagines a fisherman standing midstream with a "white wrist flicking/Flies," and ends with the warning, delivered in militaristic terms:

I go, like you, by gleam and drag

And will strike when you strike, to kill.
We're both annihilated on the fly.
You can't resist a gullet full of steel.
I will turn home fish-smelling, scaly.

The indomitable Irishry appears here in the Connemara cloth of another
more famous fisherman: the "white wrist flicking" recalls Yeats's angler
in "The Fisherman" who casts his fly with the "down-turn of his wrist."
The image of Yeats's fisherman, envisioned as "but a dream," is tinged
with the reformative zeal of a political idealism, while Heaney's angler,
who returns home "fish-smelling, scaly," seems unavoidably stained by
the long struggle such an idealism eventually entailed. With a foreboding
and characteristically Yeatsian timeliness, "The Fisherman" first ap-
peared in *Poetry* in February 1916, two months before the Easter upris-
ing in Dublin; the realistic appraisals of Heaney's poem, appearing at the
height of the violent demonstrations in Belfast and Derry, stand in
opposition to the unsullied yearning of his forebear's lyric.

Their opposing stances are mediated by the pastoral tradition. If the
Crabbean revision, the antipastoral, finds its distant forebear in Spenser's
generically oriented skepticisms, then what ultimately separates the two
traditions—and what separates pastoral from antipastoral—is their dif-
fering "sense of place," a phrase that has obvious repercussions for
descriptive poetry. Heaney has fashioned clear ideas concerning his own
sense of place, and we will turn to them presently. Modern literary
historians have reserved the term "antipastoral" for the poetry of the late
eighteenth and early nineteenth centuries, a time when many of the major
novelists were concerning themselves with the hard times and "real
picture of the poor," to use Crabbe's phrase. Antipastoral writing often
seems the poetic partner to fictional realism. Crabbe had sensed much
earlier that pastoral conventions were inadequate to represent the rural
society of late eighteenth-century England, and when such representa-
tion became the purpose of the poetry, the genre seemed woefully ill-
equipped to carry out its new mission. To such a notion Puttenham would
have undoubtedly replied that pastoral writing was never intended for
this kind of representation. He would have argued that because realism
was never an integral feature of the pastoral tradition, Crabbe's arrival
signals the dissolution of that tradition—Crabbe had come with the
hobnailed truth. His revelations are fired by a moral necessity:

> I grant indeed that fields and flocks have charms
> For him that graze or for him that farms;
> But, when amid such pleasing scenes I trace
> The poor laborious natives of the place,
> And see the mid-day sun, with fervid ray,
> On their bare heads and dewy temples play;
> While some, with feebler heads and fainter hearts,
> Deplore their fortune, yet sustain their parts:
> Then shall I dare these real ills to hide
> In tinsel trappings of poetic pride?[17]

Essentially, Crabbe is possessed by a double vision; on one hand, his writing shows a sincere enthusiasm for the charms of the country, while, on the other, his social conscience moves him to reveal the real ills of the English peasant farmer. The keen edge of factuality sharpens his revelation—the policy of enclosure brought ruin to many peasant farmers—and this quest for an abrasive realism figures prominently in Heaney's early work. Exhaustive in their particularity, his descriptions of digging, thatching, and churning are often left to stand alone, without interpretation or commentary. "To get them true," as Heaney puts it in "The Seed Cutters" from *North,* was always his first intention, and his portrayals of a Catholic boyhood spent in rural Northern Ireland represent acts of defiance in themselves. To resist the idealizing myths and conventions of formal pastoral, the poet compiles his data sheet, describing the facts and figures of his village with a passionate dispassion.

Crabbe's reformist airs, instructive as they may be, give his poetry in *The Village* a censorious tone that repels the modern reader. His poetry continually resides in the commonplace, insisting on the quotidian realities. A community viewed in the light of its distinctive detail is a community reconstructed according to the viewer's sense of place, an important idea for Heaney. This is not to say that Heaney's relation to the pastoral tradition is essentially identical to Crabbe's; reacting to the neoclassical work of Pope, Crabbe attacked the formal conventions of the genre, redesigning his descriptive methods to suit his own aims and intentions. Antipastoral writing, as suggested earlier, might profitably be seen as part of a larger movement, particularly obvious in nineteenth-century fiction, toward literary realism. The tendency toward social commentary and perhaps even toward ethical revision was present in Virgil, and the stylistic changes that took place in pastoral writing toward the end of the eighteenth century have their origins in this same revisionary urge. Heaney's version of pastoral, although not directly influenced by Crabbe's work, develops in the same climate of particularized description that distinguishes much antipastoral poetry. However, Heaney has evolved techniques of description and narration whose insinuative powers, when taken in conjunction with the work's explicitly rural subject matters, preserve in the late twentieth century the pastoral's distinct and tensioned awareness of its own social context, of its ability, as Puttenham claimed, to "insinuate and glance at greater matters."

One of the unspoken and continually changing concerns of pastoral writing derives from the sense of place implicit in each work. This sense of place, whether refined by the idealized Virgilian landscape or sharpened by the more concrete aspects of Crabbe's village, accounts for much of the genre's development over the centuries. What is meant by this ubiquitous phrase, "sense of place"? Irish writers can lay claim to a specificity in their definition that others cannot; they have at their disposal a genre of sorts called *dinnseanchas,* a form more organized and purposeful than the occasional eponymous literature of other countries. As Heaney describes it in an essay entitled "The Sense of Place," the purpose of this genre is to fashion "poems and tales which relate the original meanings of place names and constitute a form of mythological etymology." Earlier in the same essay, Heaney sketches out his ideas on his own sense of place: "I think there are two ways in which place is known and cherished, two ways which may be complementary but which are just as likely to be antipathetic. One is lived, illiterate and unconscious, the other learned, literate and conscious. In the literary sensibility, both are likely to co-exist in a conscious and unconscious tension. . . . ." Obviously, Heaney is formulating a definition much broader and more generally conceived than that of the *dinnseanchas.* He is concerned here, in his own words, with "the relationship between a literature and a locale," with the protean appearances of specific places and place-names in a writer's work.[18] Interviewed by James Randall for *Ploughshares,* Heaney spoke of his earliest influences, and he relates a story that illustrates how his own sense of place, both in its "lived" and "learned" senses, took shape:

> I remember getting Kavanagh's work for the first time. . . . And I read *The Great Hunger,* that was a thrill to me. Suddenly my own background was appearing in a book I was reading. And then I remember the day I opened Ted Hughes's *Lupercal* in the Belfast Public Library. And [there] was a poem called "View of a Pig" and in my childhood we'd killed pigs on the farm, and I'd seen pigs shaved, hung up, and so

on. So again, suddenly, the matter of contemporary poetry was the material of my own life. I had had some notion that modern poetry was far beyond the likes of me—there was Eliot and so on—so I got this thrill out of trusting my own background. . . .[19]

"There was Eliot and so on"—a phrase that shows how thoroughly Eliot still exemplified "modern poetry" for a budding writer in England and Ireland during the early 1960s. To the young Heaney, Hughes's slaughtered pig, "a poundage of pork and lard," struck a more responsive chord than Eliot's river, that "strong brown god" lying somewhere between the Mississippi and the Styx. The work of Kavanagh and Hughes represented for Heaney the "literate and conscious" sensibilities fashioned from an "illiterate and unconscious" background very similar to his own. Kavanagh and Hughes had come to give Heaney metaphors for poetry; in the rooms of the Belfast Public Library, they provided an example of a poet who had discovered forceful subject matters in a rural subculture and successfully exploited its rich trove of images.

Once Heaney had read Hughes and Kavanagh, he began more clearly to visualize the special contours of his own experience. In the early stages of molding into poetry a version of Catholic, rural Northern Ireland, the most fundamental utensils, or clothes, or tools, if the poet "gets them true," provide fodder for a poem—anything that distinguishes the less prominent culture from the dominant one becomes eligible. Kavanagh's *The Great Hunger* is, in one sense, both poetry and sociology. Many of Heaney's early poems, brimming over with what seem factual reports from the farm, are replies or challenges, in effect, to the English literary hegemony.

Potato digging, for example, would seem a dangerous subject for Irish writers; Heaney's treatment of the national tuber emphasizes the visual images presented by laborers in the field. From *Death of a Naturalist,* "At a Potato Digging" begins:

A mechanical digger wrecks the drill,
Spins up a dark shower of roots and mould.
Labourers swarm in behind, stoop to fill
Wicker creels. Fingers go dead in the cold.
Like crows attacking crow-black fields, they stretch
A higgledy line from hedge to headland. . . .

The opening verses of Kavanagh's "The Great Hunger" provide both the literary and the cultural background for Heaney's gambit:

> Clay is the word and clay is the flesh
> Where the potato-gatherers like mechanised scarecrows move
> Along the side-fall of the hill . . .
> Here crows gabble over worms and frogs. . . .[20]

The laborers of Kavanagh's poem are compared to "mechanised scarecrows," while in Heaney's poem "mechanical diggers" actually work the drills, a grim literalization of the older poet's simile. Kavanagh's crows, actual and scavenging, become the object of Heaney's simile, balancing the link of associations between the two poems. The Irish Famine of 1849 towers imposingly throughout Heaney's poem, but Heaney avoids the burdensome abstractions that regularly attend discussions, even poetic treatments, of national tragedies. Instead, Heaney narrows his focus, refining his sense of place to an obsessive level of particularity. He describes the potato:

> Flint-white, purple. They lie scattered
> like inflated pebbles. Native
> to the black hutch of clay
> where the halved seed shot and clotted
> these knobbed and slit-eyed tubers seem
> the petrified hearts of drills. Split
> by the spade, they show white as cream.

Nowhere in "The Great Hunger" does Kavanagh describe the potato. Heaney's insistent sense of particularity accounts in many ways for his equally insistent, equally Irish sense of place. Heaney's cold potatoes are not Tityrus's ripe apples, but the insistence on obliquely depicting a national calamity through a highly stylized description of an important element of the rural landscape provides an essential link to traditional pastoral.

Much in Heaney's first two collections shimmers with the kind of archaeological vividness associated with ancient objects displayed artfully under neon lights. Fired by the examples of Hughes and Kavanagh, Heaney moves through familiar terrain and holds up spades, frogs, pitchforks, churns, jam-pots, crocks, cuds, udders, and kettles, joyfully claiming them as subjects for his verse. Each reclamation becomes an act of defiance, a way of writing against the grain of Eliot's vastly assimilative modernism. As a result, a simple assertion drawn from everyday life is often enough to begin a poem:

I was six when I first saw kittens drown.
Dan Taggart pitched them, "the scraggy wee shits,"
Into a bucket, a frail metal sound,

Soft paws scraping like mad. But their tiny din
Was soon soused. They were slung on the snout
Of the pump and the water pumped in.
("The Early Purges")

The poem gained a degree of notoriety in Ireland in late 1970; in Heaney's words, "some M.P. scolded it for being on an exam paper. . . ."[21] The violence of the poem combined with Dan Taggart's homely bluntness offended the politician who, in turn, most likely feared that what offended him might influence other, perhaps younger, readers. But the poem exemplifies Heaney's love of anecdote, one of the qualities most characteristic of his early writing. Such narrative poetry, dependent upon the discursive characteristics of language, allows the writer to embody within the story the distinctive psychological and emotional inflections of his region. For Heaney storytelling becomes a way of fleshing out his sense of place, of introducing to the literary hierarchy new perspectives and attitudes—simple narrative becomes a form of cultural enshrinement. And this enshrinement depends upon an element that is native to the tradition yet intolerant of the social criticisms of Duck or Crabbe—the art of pastoral celebration.

When Crabbe decided to paint the "real picture of the poor," he did not celebrate the way of life that he detailed. Celebration of the simplicity and innocence offered by the country life had been an essential, if occasionally satirized, feature of pastoral writing since its inception. But Crabbe intended to startle and accuse. *The Village* was meant to be read as an indictment not only of the pastoral tradition that he had inherited from Pope and the eighteenth century but also as an exposé of the living conditions in rural England at the time. Crabbe's sense of place, then, is loudly reformative in its aim; Crabbe intends to dismantle the myths surrounding the countryside and the life it fostered, and to the degree that his condemnations are explicit and simplistic, his verse lacks the pastoral's insinuative powers, the particular complexity of tone needed to celebrate the downtrodden culture that he is saving.

Yet there are other writers generally assigned to the tradition who do not regularly take the extreme position that has become accepted as the antipastoral's trademark. John Clare's work, for example, celebrates as well as laments, and his work not only occupies an exalted position in Heaney's estimation, but it also provides an important precursor to Heaney's own version of pastoral. Though Clare's early poems often echo the mannered quality of Thomson's *The Seasons*, he sustained throughout his career, even after the enclosure of Helpston, his village, an enthusiasm for observing and recording the minutest aspects of rural life, a quality already observed in Heaney's "At a Potato Digging." Clare's sensibility was ideally suited to develop the pastoral tradition after it had been shorn of its classical conventions; he invigorated a chore boy's knowledge of agriculture and animal husbandry with a "soul enchanting poesy," as he calls it in "The Progress of Rhyme."[22] This is Romantic argot, and it blemishes Clare's work whenever he ranges beyond earshot of his essentially dialectal idiom, but in his best work—a poem like "The Lament of Swordy Well," which Heaney has enthusiastically proclaimed "one of the best poems of its century"[23]—Clare, like Heaney, draws from his particularized, rural descriptions the larger social and political implications. This characteristic, an unimpeachable element of pastoral writing, forms one of the strongest links between the version of pastoral developed by Clare in the nineteenth century and the one inherited by Heaney a century and a half later.

Clare's scenery derives as surely as Crabbe's and Heaney's from realistic description, but in Clare's work this authenticity is as likely to celebrate its subjects as to lament them. Intuitively concerned with the actual labors of a thresher, Clare insists on the sobering authenticity associated with antipastoral, but further develops the celebratory strain heard in the traditional literature of the genre. If the classical pastoral favored the generalizing aspects of its conventions, particularly in its portrayal of articulate shepherds wandering through idealized landscapes, it had nevertheless evolved an elaborate system of implication and insinuation, so that every blithely happy Tityrus encountered Meliboeus, dispossessed of his land. Both Clare and Heaney avoid the constricting conventions of the classical pastoral, and their carefully detailed descriptions of farm life would often seem to conjure up the reformative airs of the antipastoral. But censoriousness has no place in their verse. Cultural pride always precedes cultural equality, and in Clare's work this note of rural celebration, derived from the classical pastoral, combines with an exhaustive attention to realistic detail, derived from the antipastoral, to form a tradition in pastoral writing that reappears most vividly in Heaney's early work.

However far a particular poem may stray from the confines of traditional pastoral literature, a concern for the rural livelihood often orders the verse at its most fundamental level. As a young man, Heaney had doubted that a life confined to a small family farm in Northern Ireland would ever provide the requisite material that Eliot's influential program seemed to prescribe as the stuff of a *biographia literaria*. Clare, too, experienced similar doubts, but in his verse the apologetic note often combines with the classical formula of invocation in which the poet's declaration of unworthiness seemed most often to attract the muse's favor. Nonetheless, a substantial portion of Clare's hesitations records his sincere doubts about the possibility of a peasant farmer becoming a poet. Clare's combination of a serious occupational anxiety with the formulaic tones of the classical invocation provide, as we will see, the precedent for understanding the odd mixture of veneration and bravado that surfaces in "Digging," one of Heaney's earliest and most popular poems.

"The Progress of Rhyme," although not one of Clare's strongest poems, reveals several essential elements of his aesthetics, a term applied with a measure of reservation to a writer whose opinions on his art seem as unfettered as his often seem. Several attitudes permeate the poem, several voices, and the least persuasive of them is the voice of the glib paean:

> O soul enchanting poesy
> Thoust long been all the world with me
> When poor thy presence grows my wealth
> When sick thy visions gives me health
> When sad thy sunny smile is joy
> And was from een a tiney boy[24]

Poesies that enchant souls have become for modern readers the beacon light of an insular Romanticism. The poem vacillates between an unbridled enthusiasm and a persistent hesitation, and this itself is a pastoral theme: the "uncouth swain" of "Lycidas," who wrote with "forc'd fingers rude," exhibits the most illustrious, if contrived, diffidence that English pastoral writing offers. The following passage recalls Heaney, the young and hesitant poet, who had lumped Eliot and modern poetry together and considered the whole affair beyond his capabilities:

> All else was but a proud decree
> The right of bards and nought to me

> A title that I dare not claim
> And hid it like a private shame
> I whispered aye and felt a fear
> To speak aloud tho' none was near
> I dreaded laughter more then [sic] blame
> And dare not sing aloud for shame[25]

Earlier in the poem, Clare had spoken of his "humble dress" and asked himself if he "might have a right to happiness/And sing as well as greater men." And toward the end of the poem, when he remarks that "the polished was not mine to know," Clare's anxiety, like Heaney's, becomes in the broadest sense of the word existential. In Derry or Helpston, they each are asking, what might possibly qualify as subjects for poetry? The early work of the two writers returns an implicit answer to that question, and in both cases the same material that would have inspired Crabbe's pessimism enables Heaney and Clare to resurrect their culture with a note of defiant pride. Such subversive ironies have long played a distinguished role in pastoral poetry.

This note of defiant pride pervades Clare's work inoffensively because it never argues for its own legitimacy. When Clare writes in "The Progress of Rhyme" that "My harp tho simple was my own/When I was in the fields alone," his words have more the confident resolution of a fact than the ardent persuasion of an argument. Occasionally this pride in country affairs—or the guilt that arises from neglecting them—can frustrate the literary energies; two lines from Heaney's "Digging," which he has called a "big, coarse-grained navvy of a poem,"[26] recall the following couplet in Clare's "The Progress of Rhyme": "I felt and shunned the idle vein/Laid down the pen and toiled again. . . ." The couplet that begins Heaney's poem issues from the confident resolve following a similar doubt: "Between my finger and my thumb/The squat pen rests; snug as a gun."

Both writers are at times distrustful of their art; several lines later, Heaney uncovers the central anxiety of the poem and presents the one insight that orders its broad range of emotions. It appears as the last line of the quatrain:

> The cold smell of potato mould, the squelch and slap
> Of soggy peat, the curt cuts of an edge
> Through living roots awaken in my head.
> But I've no spade to follow men like them.

Such verse, pitting intellectual endeavor against physical labor, recalls the worker's distrust of "book-learning," the mutual skepticisms harbored between the "polished" poet and the peasant poet. When Heaney admits, perhaps confesses, that he has "no spade to follow men like them," he feels a touch of sadness, the kind of occupational tension that accompanies a change in jobs. And the peculiar vulnerability of the line stems from the poet's hesitation to claim potato mould and soggy peat as subjects for his verse. But a deeper skepticism plumbs the work, and it concerns Heaney's sense of community, his loyalty to his ancestors. In the Haffenden interview, Heaney spoke about this skepticism:

> When I was in Glanmore I thought a lot about the function of writing. Dan Jacobson said to me once, "You feel bloody well guilty about writing," and there is indeed some part of me that is entirely unimpressed by the activity, that doesn't dislike it, but it's the generations, I suppose, of rural ancestors—not illiterate, but not literary. They, in me, or I through them, don't give a damn. I don't know whether that's a good thing or a bad thing.[27]

Writers frequently disclaim what they do while doing it prolifically, a psychological ploy often meant to avoid self-consciousness. But in "Digging," Heaney develops a theme integral to his version of pastoral and to his ideas about the pastoral's political dimension. The poem, as he tells us, sprang from a recollection of walking to school and hearing the workmen say to him:

> "The pen's easily handled. It's a lot lighter than the spade. Aye, boy, it's lighter than the spade, I'm telling you." Years later when I came to write a poem about what it meant to be a poet living away out of the country I came from and the people I came from, I think I must have remembered the roadman's words about the pen and the spade.

Pastoral poetry rises, as Kermode wrote, from a "sharp difference between two ways of life, the rustic and the urban."[28] In "Digging," Heaney has refined this antithesis and pits his people's unfamiliarity with all things literary against his own poetic aspirations, aspirations that become associated with "living away out of the country." Heaney acknowledges his ancestral skepticism toward the verbal arts, a skepticism handed down by generations "not illiterate but not literary," and his poetry, which seeks to define and clarify his culture, is drawn ironically from a culture wary of the poetic endeavor. As a result, he often writes from the perspective of the domestic exile, perhaps even of the "inner émigré" who closes *North,* a perspective claimed by many writers but one that grows naturally from Heaney's pastoral. In *Station Island,* Heaney is still confronting a situation similar to the one introduced in "Digging" twenty years earlier. The poem, entitled "Making Strange," opens by sketching out the middle ground that has become so familiar to him:

> I stood between them,
> the one with his travelled intelligence
> and tawny containment,
> his speech like the twang of a bowstring,
>
> and another, unshorn and bewildered
> in the tubs of his wellingtons,
> smiling at me for help,
> faced with this stranger I'd brought him.

In these elegantly casual quatrains, Heaney assumes the position of a mediator, introducing a man from the countryside that has nourished his art to a man from the city that has appreciated it. Such a stance, in many ways, is emblematic of Heaney's career. Catholic and Protestant, North and South, Republican and Unionist, rural and urban—these are the dichotomies often associated with him, the dichotomies that some of his more stringent readers have expected him to resolve. Yet resolution, in this case, is not Heaney's concern. The resolution of larger social issues, if it arises at all in the poetry, arises from the emotional matrix of the individual author, from the ambivalences and tensions that characterize Heaney's response to the events surrounding him. Such a poem, as Paulin asserts, will embody a historical awareness that merits political analysis. The pastoral tradition, having been adapted over the centuries to acts of implication and insinuation, provides Heaney with a way of forcefully organizing a few of these dichotomies.

The early poem, "Digging," begins such an organization, and the poem's formal structure provides one of the clearest and most obvious insights into its thematic concerns. As we have noted, the poem begins with a couplet. It is octosyllabic, the measure chosen by Clare in "The Progress of Rhyme" and one of Clare's standard measures. George Saintsbury's *A History of English Prosody,* as valuable for its promenading prose style as for its polemical commandments concerning English prosody, includes a brief sketch of the octosyllabic genealogy that is still unsurpassed. He begins, as always, with an assessment of the competition:

> The decasyllable, although, as we have seen, an early if not frequent or regular product of the imposition of foot-scansion on English language, was . . . a very late comer to any considerable extent. . . . The octosyllable, on the other hand, was of the most ancient house of distinctively English—that is Middle English—poetry. It had shown itself, struggling, but holding its own, at the very birth thereof; it had steadily triumphed; it had never been cast out or held under; and, best of all, it had, from all but the earliest period, adapted itself to the two systems, uniform and equivalenced, of syllabic metring [sic]. It was thus prepared to meet any change in pronunciation, any difficulties of form; its general rhythm being so planted in the English tongue and ear that nothing could drive it out or smother it.[29]

These are extravagant claims, but they emphasize the imposing priority of the tetrameter line in English verse. The initial tetrameter couplet of the poem gives way in the second stanza to the newcomer, the decasyllabic couplet:

> Under my window, a clean rasping sound
> When the spade sinks into gravelly ground
> My father, digging. I look down
>
> Till his straining rump among the flowerbeds
> Bends low, comes up twenty years away
> Stooping in rhythm through potato drills
> Where he was digging.
>
> The coarse boot nestled on the lug, the shaft
> Against the inside knee was levered firmly.
> He rooted out tall tops, buried the bright edge deep
> To scatter new potatoes that we picked
> Loving their cool hardness in our hands.

The last line of the second stanza, however, is again listening to the octosyllabic metronome as Heaney atones for the extravagances of the longer count by returning to the older: "My father, digging. I look

33

down. . . ." Something is gained, the quiet confidence of terseness, and something is lost, the noisy confidence of elaboration, a formula that, in this early probing poem, effectively provides the structural analogy to Heaney's ambivalent attitude toward his literary aspirations. Such skepticism concerning the literary life implicitly advocates the superiority of the country life, and this dichotomy, in its several variations, forms the backbone of pastoral literature. The poem celebrates the rural life that Heaney will transform into poetry, and as his descriptions of his father at work become more detailed, more impassioned, the length of his stanzas swell. The poem in fact embodies a brief history of the English stanza— in succession appear a couplet, a tercet, a quatrain, and a quintet. The burgeoning confidence of the lines derives from the poet's gradual discovery of his subject matter, and this confidence is reflected by the stanzaic patterns. The last two stanzas move toward a quieter resolution:

> The cold smell of potato mould, the squelch and slap
> Of soggy peat, the curt cuts of an edge
> Through living roots awaken in my head.
> But I've no spade to follow men like them.

> Between my finger and my thumb
> The squat pen rests.
> I'll dig with it.

The first line of the quatrain is actually a hexameter, but it yields quickly to the regular pentameter measure that finishes the stanza. The first line of the final stanza comes to rest in the octosyllabic line, and the last two are precise halves of that measure. The shrinking line does not reflect a weakening of the will. Rather, the clipped lines, beating out the primal cadences of the language, suggest the quiet confidence that comes, in Heaney's phrase, from casting one's feeling into words. Now faltering, now surging, the poem's musical rhythms reflect the uncertainties of a young poet finding the linguistic form of his own unique sense of place. This unique sense of place—the phrase must be taken in its broadest aspect to include his people and his landscape—aligns him with the pastoral tradition, particularly the tradition reconstituted by Clare's work. The community that Heaney resurrects in his poetry is rural and Catholic, and although his is a community often under siege, he begins to respond with a dissenting voice succored by the curt, clipped accents of a modern pastoral.

"The place we occupy seems all the world":
Pastoral Revision in Clare and Heaney

In a review of an anthology of pastoral verse, Heaney identifies those authors who first attempted to reconcile the vying concerns of social realism with the exotic extravagance of pastoral convention. He commends Clare's verse highly, and the language of his commendation demonstrates how clearly he understands the fundamental changes of the tradition as it developed in the early nineteenth century:

> With Duck, Crabbe and Clare there emerges . . . a voice protesting on behalf of the agricultural labourer, who no longer appears as jocund swain or abstract Industry but as a hard-driven human being. It is a voice that has some trouble with its accent—Duck's natural country vigor is soon smoothed out and co-opted by the conventional diction of the period—and it was the unique achievement of John Clare to make vocal the regional and particular, to achieve a buoyant and authentic lyric utterance at the meeting-point between social realism and conventional romanticism.[1]

For Heaney, the "jocund swain" belongs to a "conventional romanticism," but the figure derives ultimately from the pastoral tradition. If Clare's poetry represents the happy conjunction of authenticity and celebration, two traditionally discordant elements of pastoral writing, then his work may elucidate some of the fundamental problems that distinguish Heaney's own reconciling renovations of the genre. Readers of Clare's verse become intimately familiar with the villages of Helpston, where the poet passed the first thirty-eight years of his life, and Northborough, where he pined away the next five. Clare never saw a world in a grain of sand; his verse delights in variety and prospers from surprise. He would seem a poet of indiscriminating sensibilities if it were not for the rural community, the hills, stumps, wells, pools, meadows, sparrows, and weathers that consistently organize his work.

Lurking in the word "community" is a sense of protection and confrontation, a sense of agreement concerning certain ideals and values. Sharing in a way of life that was fast fading, Clare and his community, its beliefs and practices, are consistently united in his verse against the amorphous evils of "dependence" and "enclosure." Heaney too has spoken in similar terms of his rural community, and he has emphasized the divisions and confrontations that actually solidify its self-conception:

> For if this was the country of community, it was also the realm of division. Like the rabbit pads that loop across grazing, and tunnel the soft growths under ripening corn, the lines of sectarian antagonism and affiliation followed the boundaries of the land. In the names of its fields and townlands, in their mixture of Scots and Irish and English etymologies, this side of the country was redolent of the histories of its owners.[2]

Both Clare and Heaney tirelessly recreate in their poems the daily affairs of their lives and the larger rituals that bestow on them a coherence and integrity shared by their community. The necessity of nostalgia, the binding force of human love, the pride in physical labor, in a job well done, and the peculiarly narcissistic temptation of the solitary country life—these are the new versions of old pastoral themes that allow Clare and Heaney to fashion a poetic record of their distinctive communities. And their concerns not only demonstrate the various ways in which pastoral continues, but they also point to the importance of Clare's work in understanding Heaney's early poetry.

As Paulin has argued, possession and dispossession, with one culture imposing its way on another, often determine the course of development that a language pursues.[3] The parallel between Heaney and Clare is of limited use if developed irresponsibly, but even a brief assessment of the various cultural tensions that characterize each poet's relation with the larger British community reveals striking similarities as well as illuminating differences both in their verse and their biographies. Clare was a member of the English peasantry and received little formal education; and he was never forced, as Heaney has been, to confront the cultural implications of living with a legally imposed citizenship that contradicts his deepest inclinations. Although Clare speaks for a disfranchised community in England, the question of its Englishness never arises. In Heaney's poetry, the question of nationality, both in its legal and cultural aspects, provides the background for many of his poems and essays. The fate of the pastoral during Clare's time has caused many critics to deliver its eulogy, but several of the similarities between Clare's and Heaney's verse indicate that rumors of the tradition's death have been greatly exaggerated. Crabbe's radical reaction to the classical pastoral effectively resolved Johnson's charges of incredibility, and when the voice of agricultural expertise becomes a desideratum of the tradition, pastoral writing invites the farmer, if endowed with the proper literary skills, to enter its province. The court poets, with their urban perspective, no longer shape the tradition, and the several qualities shared by Clare and Heaney—their firsthand knowledge of farm life, their sense of a community under seige, and their awareness of the pastoral's ability to glance at greater matters—become the most important elements of the genre's latest guise.

Clare was once best known for his late "asylum" poems, particularly the sonnet "I Am," but the profound resignation of those fourteen lines seems an anomalous coda to an essentially joyous body of work. Even in despondency, Clare rarely loses sight of his community. Plural both in its grammatical number and its redemptive implications, the subject "we" appears suddenly in the last line of "November," and the alienation of the preceding lines becomes a collective, ameliorating one:

> The shepherds almost wonder where they dwell
> And the old dog for his night journey stares
> The path leads somewhere but they cannot tell
> And neighbour meets with neighbour unawares
> The maiden passes close beside her cow
> And wonders on and thinks her far away
> The ploughman goes unseen behind his plough
> And seems to loose his horses half the day

37

The lazy mist creeps on in journey slow
The maidens shout and wonder where they go
So dull and dark are the november days
The lazy mist high up the evening curled
And now the morn quite hides in smokey haze
The place we occupy seems all the world

The stichomythic quality of each verse conjures a fit emblem for the loneliness felt by the various characters that wander through the poem. The "place" here is dark and claustrophobic, but its claustrophobia is mediated by a consoling quorum of shepherds, dogs, neighbors, maidens, and plowmen. Characteristically, Clare brings a shared wisdom, an innately social comfort to the conflicts shaping his poems. The peculiar lineaments of his pastoral society stand, for example, poised between Pope's idealistic, "fairer flocks" and Crabbe's gloomy, "declining swains." Whether fleeing satyrs in Arcadia or bullfrogs in Derry, poets who delve into country matters reveal attitudes, perspectives, and ideals that attempt to explain and justify their interests in these humble affairs. And, as often as not, their explanations and justifications provide a creative profile, an imaginative sociology, of the communities they envision.

But pastoral visions are opposing visions. They propose to replace one way of life with another, and although this proposition is often more an enticement than an invitation, the argumentative aspects of the work require the author to form coherent conceptions of the Iron Age currently confining the world and the Golden Age that will ascend to claim its rightful station. But not all pastoralists deal in such extremities. Yeats was the last poet to dream infectiously of Arcady, and even then "the woods of Arcady [were] dead." Speculating on the modern pastoral compromise, Heaney speaks of "the counter-cultural celebration of simpler life-styles" and wonders if such celebrations are not "continuous with the [pastoral] tradition. . . ."[4] As demonstrated earlier, Clare revived the art of pastoral celebration, and in his hands celebration becomes the mother of resistance. To praise a community is to preserve a community, guarding it against cultural assimilation, and many of the methods Clare employed to celebrate his culture were "counter-cultural," as Heaney phrases it, because they were scorned both by his publishers and patrons.

The full title of Clare's first volume reveals the subtle social biases that attended, perhaps titillated, the literary world of London: *Poems*

Descriptive of Rural Life and Scenery, by John Clare, a Northampton-shire Peasant (1820). If the poems described by the title were unable to win admiration on their own merits, then perhaps the lowly station of their creator would render them a literary curiosity. Peasant poetry has always had its niche in the English literary hierarchy, but Clare, like Stephen Duck, was formally introduced to London society, and his introductions were often founded on clever marketing strategies that took advantage of the vast economic and cultural differences that existed between the communities he embraced. After the first collection appeared, Clare, for example, received an invitation to visit Milton Hall, an estate where he had worked as a gardener, and one of his publishers, Edward Drury, sent him an appropriate peasant shirt, advising him not to arrive in his best clothes, "which are more suitable to a Squire of high degree than humble John Clare." Clare's description of the meeting is a penetrating portrayal of two distinctly different communities momentarily yoked by the literary arts:

> On the following Sunday I went and after sitting awhile in the servants hall where I could hear or drink nothing for though his Lordship sent for me and instantly explained the reason why he did not answer my letter in a quiet unaffected manner which set me at rest he told me he had heard of my poems by Parson Mossop who I have since heard took hold of every opportunity to speak against my success or poetical abilitys before the book was published . . . Lady Milton also asked me several questions and wished me to name any book that was a favourite expressing at the same time a desire to give me one but I was confounded & coud think of nothing & so I lost the present in fact I did not like to pick out a book for fear of seeming over reaching on her kindness . . . they gave me a handful of money the most I had ever possesd in my life together & I felt almost sure I should be poor no more there was seventeen pounds.[5]

Humility, kindness, charity, patronage—both the attributes and the institutions that appear in this passage are associated with the task of social reconciliation, of finding ways for the earl and peasant to converse. Before the late eighteenth century, such introductions would not have taken place; the vast changes in sensibility that had gradually fostered Crabbe's insistence on authenticity when dealing with pastoral subjects had finally fostered at Milton Hall vast changes in a lord's guest list. Clare's discomfort in the manor house, his sense of alienation, is analogous to a similar cultural alienation found in Heaney's poetry whenever he confronts the mansion of English culture. In this verse, such social confrontations are rendered by highly stylized literary techniques designed to nurture the differences that support the concept of Irish sovereignty. In "A Peacock's Feather," a poem included in *The Haw Lantern* (1987), the poet is addressing his "English niece" born and christened in Gloucestershire:

> Gloucestershire: its prospects lie
> Wooded and misty to my eye
> Whose landscape, as your mother's was,
> Is other than this mellowness
> Of topiary, lawn and brick,
> Possessed, untrespassed, walled, nostalgic.
>
> I come from scraggy farm and moss,
> Old patchworks that the pitch and toss
> Of history have left dishevelled.
> But here, for your sake, I have levelled
> My cart-track voice to garden tones,
> Cobbled the bog with Cotswold stones.

One facet of Heaney's self-portrait in this poem, that of an unshorn Irish bumpkin in an English pleasance, is nonsense; but its nonsensical aspect is less important than the argumentative strategy it depends upon, a strategy that owes much to Clare's stance of domestic exile. Poetry that addressed country affairs was often seen during Clare's time as deriving its strength from the peasantry's quaint cadences, not from its vision of Virgilian mythology. This represents a significant development in the literary history of England because it invited a large and important subculture to enjoy the privileges and powers of authorship.

Such privileges and powers, however, did not go unchecked. They never do. And the tensions that existed between Clare's version of Helpston and London's version of Clare provide a concise, if occasionally obvious, introduction to the subversive qualities of the community that he created in his verse. Patrons are either malevolent or benevolent, depending on whether they pride themselves for supporting their poets or pride their poets for accepting their patronage, and Lord Radstock, who had become one of Clare's patrons, also became one of Clare's censors. Before the second edition of *Poems Descriptive* was scheduled for publication, he was already making suggestions for revision, and these revisions were designed to maintain the sterling image of the English landed gentry. A reference, for example, to the "ploughman" as "the necessary tool of wealth and pride" was struck from "The Dawnings of Genius"; in May 1820, when the third edition was about to appear, Clare received a letter from Eliza Louisa Emmerson, another patron, who urged Clare to leave out the offensive phrases and quoted Lord Radstock as saying, "tell Clare if he has still a recollection of what I have done, and am still doing for him, he must give me unquestionable *proofs* of being that Man I would have him to be—he must expunge—expunge!"[6]

In a fit of innocuous neglect, Clare became "that Man" Radstock wished him to be by leaving the matter of expurgation entirely to his publisher, John Taylor. Writing to Clare, Taylor struck a paternal pose and warned him that a failure to comply with Radstock's wishes would endanger his patronage; he continued sagely by saying that "when the Follies of the Day are past . . . we can restore the Poems according to the earlier Editions."[7]

The formation of a literary sensibility requires, among a myriad of other things, the leisure time to develop it, and the disagreement here between poet and patron resides at one level in the various differences between the life of a Northamptonshire peasant and an English lord. But in Heaney's work, this division involves the problem of national identity, as the "parish" culture of Ireland confronts the cosmopolitan literary culture of British Northern Ireland. In a personal essay written for the Northern Irish biweekly, *Fortnight*, Heaney spoke of the two opposing cultures, "the official British culture . . . and the anthropological culture," and as in Clare's version, one represented literary sophistication, the other provincial piety:

> Moving from primary school to university, when I think back on those years I can see a similar tension. I was studying English, reading Shakespeare and Oscar Wilde and Chaucer and Dickens, considering the rhythms of the Authorized Version of the Bible and their effect on English prose, considering the tradition of courtly love, learning to find my way among the ironies and niceties of Jane Austen's vicarages, discussing Tennyson's loss of faith . . . and learning the rituals of the sherry party by attending receptions at the house of our Oxford professor. . . .

He next describes his life at home:

> Meanwhile, at the weekends and during the holidays, far from thesherry parties of Malone Road, the secretary of the local Pioneer Total

Abstinence Association was enrolling me as a probationer in the society; far from the elegances of Oscar Wilde and the profundities of Shakespeare, I was acting with the Bellaghy Dramatic Society in plays about 1798, now playing a United Irishman, a blacksmith forging pikes on a real anvil fetched from Devlin's forge at Hillhead. . . . Was I failing to live up to the aspiring literary intellectual effort when I was at home, [or] was I betraying the culture of the parish when I was at the university?[8]

Clare's poetry, to an astonishing degree, preserves the cadences, imagery, and diction that distinguished his own community, and Heaney's poetry attempts a similar preservation. But in Heaney's verse, the rural life becomes synonymous with Irish life, and the resulting tension involves more than an opposition of the rural and the urban; it involves an opposition of Irish and British. Pastoral tensions in Heaney's verse often represent national ones.

Much of Clare's and Heaney's work springs from an acute nostalgia that has a long and well-developed history in pastoral poetry. By his manipulation of one of the genre's standard themes, Clare, even in revised versions, retained a gesture of resistance. Laurence Lerner's *The Uses of Nostalgia* makes a fundamental and valuable observation about the structure of this emotion: "Any emotion can provide the impulse of a lyric poem; but nostalgia can provide its structure as well. For nostalgia posits two different times, a present and a longed-for past, and on this contrast a poem can be built."[9]

"Helpstone," one of Clare's earliest poems, relies on a diction unremarkable, even hidebound in its allegiance to a hyperbolic nostalgia:

> Thou far fled pasture long evanish'd scene
> Where nature's freedom spread the flowry green
> Where golden kingcups open'd in to view . . .
> Where lowing oxen roamd to feed at large
> And bleating there the shepherd's woolly charge
> Whose constant calls thy echoing vallies cheer'd
> Thy scenes adornd and rural life endeard
> No calls of hunger Pity's feelings wound
> Twas wanton Plenty rais'd the joyful sound
> Thy grass in plenty gave the wish'd supply

But to readers of the early nineteenth century, several of these words would have had significant and specific connotations relating to the policy of enclosure. In this early poem, Clare exhibits his deft ability to manage both political concerns and narrative integrity; the oppressive vocabularies of ideologies, the bane of a vigorous poetic diction, never mar his verse, even when addressing the notorious policies of land management prevalent during his time.

Enclosure, dating back to the twelfth century, involved the amalgamation of small farms into larger, more profitable ones. Although this practice, in one form or another, had existed for centuries, it was not until 1811 that an act of Parliament was passed "for enclosing lands in the parishes of Maxey with Deepingate, Northbourough, Glinton with Peakirk, Etton, and Helpstone."[10] The legislation exerted a far-ranging influence on the daily life of the small farmer, and Clare's poetry bears an eloquent witness to that influence. By fencing in large tracts of land that had once surrounded the small villages of the English countryside, landowners destroyed the sense of uninhibited freedom that many of the villagers shared. When Clare speaks of "freedom," and the oxen that "roamd to feed at large," and the "wanton plenty," and the grass that "in plenty gave the wish'd supply," he is not manufacturing an otherworldly myth of a past Golden Age. Clare's nostalgia, like other literary nostalgias, contrasts the present with the past, but unlike Pope—to take an obvious example—whose backward glances were directed toward a time as remote in history as in credibility, Clare speaks of an immediate past. The diction of Clare's early work is culled from Thomson's *The Seasons,* and although Clare energetically confronts the issue of enclosure in this and other poems, he often preserves many of the ameliorating niceties of Thomson's language. As a result, the confrontations between landowner and peasant, between the different communal concerns, never become the exclusive focus of the poetry.

This vocabulary of nostalgia, however, was so thoroughly embedded in Clare's work that even Lord Radstock's careful excisions, self-protective and prissy, could not temper its protests. By relying on words which, seemingly bound to eighteenth-century landscape descriptions, assumed an aggressive posture when read within the context of the relevant parliamentary legislation, Clare preserved in his verse a strain of pressing unrest. The implicit resistance of his poetry does not simply register the voice of a single poet, but the ruminations of an entire community. Clare emerges, for the modern reader, as the spokesman for this community, and because the patrons and publishers who encouraged his work often belonged to the financial establishment that destroyed the social and cultural dynamics of his village, he was forced to develop a poetry of a subtly subversive sophistication. Much of Clare's accomplishment lies in his founding of a poetic style that accurately captures the distinctive inflections of his community. Heaney's verse, extraordinarily urbane, nonetheless relies on strategies and techniques that Clare employed in the early nineteenth century when the pastoral was undergoing its severest modifications.

Heaney's interest in etymology, his ability to salvage poems from a word's history, are well known. But his insistence on preserving the spoken language of his native Derry countryside provides both an integral part of his program and an important link with Clare's verse. Traditionally, the science of etymology has largely concerned morphology and semantics, but Heaney's engaged etymologies bring a concern for pronunciation, for the community's verbal music to bear on the discipline. From *Wintering Out*, the title of the following poem, "Fodder," appears in its dialectal version in the second line:

> Or, as we said,
> *fother,* I open
> my arms for it
> again. But first
>
> to draw from the tight
> vise of a stack
> the weathered eaves
> of the stack itself
>
> falling at your feet,
> last summer's tumbled
> swathes of grass
> and meadowsweet
>
> multiple as loaves
> and fishes, a bundle
> tossed over half-doors
> or into mucky gaps.
>
> These long nights
> I would pull hay
> for comfort, anything
> to bed the stall.

A carefully modulated progression of rural imagery culminates in the "loaves/and fishes" of the fourth quatrain, a simple but redemptive repast that speaks of abundance and security, comforts that the poet sorely misses in the last stanza. Essentially, "Fodder" is a nostalgia piece, like much pastoral writing, but its insistence on beginning with the local pronunciation of the word reveals another link with Clare's verse. The first two lines of Clare's sonnet, "Winter Evening," might pass for lines from Heaney's first book, *Death of a Naturalist,* so similar are they in subject matter and diction. Yet what is most interesting about them is the appearance of the word "fother," phonetically—and naively—transcribed in Clare's poem to match his own pronunciation of the term:

> The crib stock fothered—horses suppered up
> And cows in sheds all littered down in straw
> The threshers gone the owls are left to whoop
> The ducks go waddling with distended craw

The title of Heaney's poem, "Fodder," preserves the conventional orthography, while the alternative pronunciation fondly recited in the second line initiates a kind of linguistic independence both from standard English and, as a result, from the English community. By emphasizing the nuances of the spoken language, Heaney is able to portray more fully the rural culture that he is introducing to the Anglo-Irish tradition. His dialectal rendition of "fother" is pervaded by a wistful nostalgia, a linguistic nostalgia in effect, and one that implicitly envies Clare's unabashed and untutored transcription. In one sense, Clare's poems with their naive simplicity and provincial devotion represent Heaney's longed-for past. And nostalgia, as Lerner suggested, belongs inherently to the pastoral tradition, informing the poet's verse with an enameling vision of the past.[11] Clare's work, with its resistive and provincial integrity, provides a revealing tradition, a palimpsest, for much of Heaney's poetry.

Different influences and different literary genealogies structure the work of each poet. Where Heaney's diction acknowledges and assimilates sources that range from Dante through Shakespeare to Paul Muldoon, a young contemporary Irish poet, Clare's begins in Thomson's *The Seasons,* occasionally retains the biblical cadences that he heard as a child, and ends having developed an idiom distinguished by its defining, regional dialect. Yet both poets, when describing similar incidents, rely on similar imagery. A brief survey of their short lyrics illustrates how

Heaney's verse often offers modernized renditions of themes that engaged Clare as he reconstructed his rural community. Love and, to some extent, love poetry transcend economic hardship. Here is Clare describing a surprise meeting with "nelly" in a poem entitled "Song":

> One gloomy eve I roamd about
> Neath oxeys hazel bowers
> While timid hares were daring out
> To crop the dewy flowers
> And soothing was the scene to me
> Right placid was my soul
> My breast was calm as summers sea
> When waves forget to roll
>
> But short was evens placid smile
> My startld soul to charm
> When nelly lightly skipt the stile
> Wi milk pail on her arm
> One carless look on me she flung
> As bright as parting day
> And like a hawk from covert sprung
> Id pounce my peace away

The bawdy pun on "peace" is analogous to a similar maneuver in one of Heaney's early lyrics. The second stanza of "Twice Shy," from *Death of a Naturalist,* begins with the "traffic holding its breath," the kind of peaceful vignette that quickly reveals its sexual tensions:

> Her scarf *à la* Bardot,
> In suede flats for the walk,
> She came with me one evening
> For air and friendly talk.
> We crossed the quiet river,
> Took the embankment walk.
>
> Traffic holding its breath,
> Sky a tense diaphragm:
> Dusk hung like a backcloth
> That shook where a swan swam,
> Tremulous as a hawk
> Hanging deadly, calm.

> A vacuum of need
> Collapsed each hunting heart
> But tremulously we held
> As hawk and prey apart,
> Preserved classic decorum,
> Deployed our talk with art . . .
>
> So, chary and excited
> As a thrush linked on a hawk,
> We thrilled to the March twilight
> With nervous childish talk:
> Still waters running deep
> Along the embankment walk.

The theme of rapacious love holds a venerable place in English literature, and the hawk provides the obvious, even predictable, symbol of the aggressor. Yet both poets are held "tremulously . . . apart" from the objects of their desire, and titillation, whose peculiar joy lies in the anticipation of other joys, provides the erotic dimension of the pastoral vision, of the desire for the distant and unattainable pastoral world. Although Heaney's poem obviously occurs in a city or town and Clare's in the country, both poets become entranced pedestrians, innocent travelers waylaid by love, as the poems end. Nelly, skipping "wi milk pail on her arm," represents the quintessential milk maiden, and her seemingly innocent nonchalance piques her powers as a pastoral seductress. The woman in Heaney's poem shares none of the milk maiden's simplicity, and the reference to Bardot and the "suede flats" further distinguishes her from her rural ancestor. Yet the idyllic geographies of the poems, the scenery that stands just beyond the principal characters, preserve the kind of dramatic tensions associated with nostalgia and the pastoral tradition. Smooth waters undulate calmly in both lyrics, one within the poem's setting, the other within the context of a simile. The "classic decorum" of Heaney's poem aptly describes the tranquil, picture-book quality of Clare's opening scene—only in an Arcadia about to be razed by the enthralling powers of love would "hazel bowers" abound, "timid hares" gambol, and "dewy flowers" flourish. Neither poem moves to a monumental conclusion. Both are satisfied to represent the hard and obdurate differences between a sobering, innocent love and a nostalgic love of innocence.

Images and ideas in other poems from *Death of a Naturalist* recall similar images and ideas from Clare's work, yet it is well to remember

47

that in the vast, amorphous tradition of pastoral writing certain subjects will be shared coincidentally. And these coincidences do not necessarily form the basis for making elucidating comparisons between the two poets—pastoral writing is distinguished by its characteristic attitude toward the country life, not simply by a depiction of that life. For example, Clare's "Morning Harvest" and Heaney's "Follower" concern various forms of manual labor. Yet their common topics do not form the strongest link between them; they are united by the governing emotion that interprets them. Heaney's poem begins with a paean to his father, the plower:

> My father worked with a horse-plough
> His shoulders globed like a full sail strung
> Between the shafts and the furrow.
> The horses strained at his clicking tongue.
>
> An expert. He would set the wing
> And fit the bright steel-pointed sock.
> The sod rolled over without breaking.

The poem turns quickly from paean to confession:

> I stumbled in his hob-nailed wake,
> Fell sometimes on the polished sod;
> Sometimes he rode me on his back
> Dipping and rising to his plod.
>
> I wanted to grow up and plough,
> To close one eye, stiffen my arm.
> All I ever did was follow
> In his broad shadow round the farm.

Plowing, an innocuous labor, becomes in this poem a rite of passage carrying with it the pressures and expectations that attend the maturational ceremonies of any community. In "The Harvest Morning," Clare depicts a "boy" involved in a similar situation:

> Upon the Waggon now with eager bound
> The lusty picker wirls the rustling sheaves
> Or ponderous resting creaking fork aground

> Boastful at once whole shocks o' barley heaves
> The loading boy revengefull inly greaves
> To find his unmatch'd strength and power decay
> Tormenting horns his garments inter weaves
> Smarting and sweating 'neath the sultry day
> Wi muttering curses stung he mauls the heaps away

Milking, harvesting, shoeing, herding, foddering—whatever the chore, and whether in Virgil or Crabbe, these activities abound. Clare, however, transforms these traditional labors into credible poetic fictions by showing how they are woven into the emotional fabric of the community. For Clare and Heaney, chores represent neither the idyllic pastimes of a rural utopia nor the unalleviated drudgeries of a suffering peasantry— they are seamlessly intertwined with the maturational process of a young boy, one of many traditions that binds the community together. Such balance, such equanimity in dealing with the laborer's life distinguishes Clare's work, and in Heaney's hands the careful attention devoted to the emotional consequences of plowing a field accounts for his sense of community, the feeling of social cohesion that permeates his early poems. The various landscapes of Heaney's youth seem at once gilded by nostalgic recollection and particularized by the harsh assertiveness of the local detail, the "clicking tongue" of Heaney's father. The peculiar tension created by this adroit portraiture derives from the pastoral tradition.

Yet the poetry of both Clare and Heaney shows a clear awareness of the traditional themes that allowed the pastoral poet to move effortlessly from description to speculation. And solitude, its pleasures and pains, was a favorite subject. Shepherds in classical and Renaissance literature lolled under olive trees singing and playing to one another, and because one shepherd often heard another shepherd rapt in solitary entertainment, shepherds of the literature were seen to be lonely figures. Narcissism poses the traditional and enticing danger to the poetic mind, and Clare was aware of its special seductions. In "Reccolections after a Ramble," he recalls,

> Then I stood to pause again
> Retrospection sighd and smild
> Musing 'tween a joy and pain
> How I acted when a child
> When by clearing brooks Ive bin

When the painted sky was given
Thinking if I tumbld in
I should fall direct to heaven

Clare's iconoclastic imagination revels in literalizing a version of the narcissistic metaphor—confusing the reflection of the thing for the thing itself, Narcissus leans so precipitously over the bank that he tumbles in, falling "direct to heaven." Heaney's "Personal Helicon," which closes his first collection, ultimately refuses to indulge the narcissistic fantasy as well:

As a child, they could not keep me from wells
And old pumps with buckets and windlasses.
I loved the dark drop, the trapped sky, the smells
Of waterweed, fungus and dank moss.

One, in a brickyard, with a rotted board top.
I savoured the rich crash when a bucket
Plummeted down at the end of a rope.
So deep you saw no reflection in it.

A shallow one under a dry stone ditch
Fructified like any aquarium.
When you dragged out long roots from the soft mulch
A white face hovered over the bottom.

Others had echoes, gave back your own call
With a clean new music in it. . . .

Now, to pry into roots, to finger slime,
To stare, big-eyed Narcissus, into some spring
Is beneath all adult dignity. I rhyme
To see myself, to set the darkness echoing.

A crisp march by the wells and springs of Heaney's childhood, the poem comes to rest in the post-Freudian age, substituting the indulgent fantasy of writing prosodically formal verse for the fantastic indulgence of mirror-watching. And finally, to return to "Reccolections after a Ramble," the country life receives its clearest treatment as a source of strong poetic inspiration; the terminology of the passage is explicitly martial, and the term "rurallity," although descended from its medieval Latin root *ruralitas,* does not figure prominently in the language until the early eighteenth century. Here, Clare extends the word's previously limited range to include the connotation of resistance and strength:

> Rurallity I dearly love thee
> Simple as thy numbers run
> Epics song may soar above thee
> Still thy sweetness yields to none
> Cots to sing and woods and vales
> Tho its all thy reed can do
> These with nature shall prevail
> When epics war harps broke in two

Overt and unabashed transformations of springs, wells, and woods into metaphors for the creative processes do not stand out as strikingly new revisions of old tropes. But they point to a common feature of Clare's and Heaney's pastoral. In both cases, the rural life, or "rurallity" as Clare calls it, instigates a meditation subtly but unmistakably assertive. For Clare, "nature shall prevail/When epics war harps broke in two," and for Heaney, less martial in his orientation, the ascension of "adult dignity" has "set the darkness echoing." Whether war harps are breaking or adult dignity is ascending, the results are the same—the song of rural inspiration prevails. In neither poet does the countryside appear as a retreat, the kind of Horatian refuge where farm life is a life of cultivated leisure; and this active recruitment of an aggressive rural imagery represents not only one of the central stylistic traits shared by Clare and Heaney but also a forceful deployment of one of the pastoral's essential features, that of insinuation. The intricate, even oppressive, network of literary associations that attends these springs and wells accounts for the artificiality of the verse. But the assertive vigor of the imagery effectively revises the conventional posture of the carefree shepherd entranced by his pipings, one of the tradition's oldest vignettes. And it does so by showing how these conventional images, if properly handled, can be coaxed to represent the silent communities that have remained outside of pastoral writing.

Throughout *Death of a Naturalist* and *Door Into the Dark,* Heaney endeavors to define his own community, to register the proper intonations that will preserve a measure of authenticity in his portrayals. Marital love, maturation, and the pursuit of self-knowledge—these are a few of the consolidating rituals enshrined by most communities, and Heaney's early poetry renders them faithfully. This concern for authenticity—and its attendant concern, credibility—occupied an increasingly prominent place in the minds of those who wrote and criticized pastoral poetry. For Johnson, the lack of authenticity found in "Lycidas" made the poem incredible—neither King nor Milton ever "batt'ned" a flock in his life. Yet when this notion of authenticity began to influence the writers of pastoral in the late eighteenth and early nineteenth centuries, the phrase "antipastoral" becomes a suitable one because for Duck and Crabbe authenticity meant telling the horrible truth—no other truth would do. Heaney in Ireland, like Clare in England, avoids these stylistic and conceptual extremities and discovers a countryside in the North as vivid in its topography as its villagers are distinctive in their aggressive cultural allegiances.

A young poet's early work often bears the indelible imprint of its influences, and the style and diction of Heaney's first attempts to portray his boyhood life on a farm in County Derry owe much to the work of Keats, Hopkins, Kavanagh, Frost, and Hughes; Heaney freely admits this.[12] In its infancy, pastoral literature demanded the "rude speeches" of a shepherd, but in the course of its development it lost these formal requirements, and the designation "pastoral" now conjures up images and themes instead of words and phrases. Yet the contrapuntal music of Heaney's poetic diction often mirrors the essential tension of pastoral writing. In an interview with John Haffenden, the poet speaks revealingly about the work of Ted Hughes and about the social and political implications of poetic style:

> I think his [Hughes's] energy comes out in the quality of the diction, powerful, violent diction, and there's a kind of anger at work. Hughes's voice, I think, is in rebellion against a certain kind of demeaned, mannerly voice . . . I mean, the voice of a generation— the Larkin voice, the Movement voice, even the Eliot voice, the Auden voice—the manners of that speech, the original voices behind that poetic voice, are those of literate English middle-class culture, and I think Hughes's great cry and call and bawl is that English language and English poetry is longer and deeper and rougher than that.[13]

The important stylistic affinities that Heaney's work shares with Hughes's work have occupied Blake Morrison in his concise study of Heaney's poetry, and they need not be rehearsed here.[14] Heaney's perception of Hughes's stylistic project, that it was conceived linguistically as a type of "rebellion" against the middle-class culture of England, reveals a similar sensibility behind his own rough diction. The opening stanza of "Churning Day" from *Death of a Naturalist* exhibits the intrusive alliteration and assonance that resist the mellifluous measures of the Wordsworthian tradition of blank verse:

> A thick crust, coarse-grained as limestone rough-cast,
> hardened gradually on top of the four crocks
> that stood, large pottery bombs, in the small pantry.
> After the hot brewery of gland, cud and udder
> cool porous earthenware fermented the buttermilk
> for churning day, when the hooped churn was scoured
> with plumping kettles and the busy scrubber
> echoed daintily on the seasoned wood.
> It stood then, purified, on the flagged kitchen floor.

Like Hughes, Heaney forges a poem here whose music is as assertive as its diction is arresting. The three quickly syncopated beats of "gland, cud and udder" and the longer, more liquid phrase that follows, "cool porous earthenware," embody in its loose five-stress line the confrontational aspect of pastoral writing, of opposing one culture to another. In *Poetry as Discourse,* Anthony Easthope speaks of the ideological aspects of pentameter's domination of English verse. Referring to Roland Barthes, who argues that the form of a discourse often seeks to "naturalize" itself as myth, thereby disclaiming its ideological implication, Easthope suggests that pentameter has affected a similar charade because "it seeks to nestle all but invisibly in an equivalence with poetry itself." Heaney's verse in this poem, with its stresses and alliterative patterns crowded together, resists, even revises, the smoother cadences of iambic pentameter, a form whose most conservative interpretation would scorn the noisy recalcitrance of Heaney's line. By lavishing such care on churning butter, a subject obviously repellent to "the Larkin voice, the Movement voice, even the Eliot voice, [and] the Auden voice," Heaney locates a subject matter both faithful to its rural community and resistant to the "English middle-class."[15] Ironically, Clare's own verse, less schooled, more dependent on the dialect of his region than Heaney's verse, makes a similarly rebellious, equally joyous noise in the face of the imposing tradition. And this artful irregularity of Clare's verse, a result of his translating conventional pastoral imagery into his own idiosyncratic rhythms, represents the historical tradition that most elucidates the pastoral aspects of Heaney's early poetry.

Clare's poetry exhaustively catalogs the quotidian realities of farm life, but in his best verse these insistent details, rather than frustrate the mythopoeic energies, provide him with opportunities for reordering older myths, such as the Narcissus legend examined earlier. And when Heaney's poetry, especially that of the first two books, attempts to transcend its own particularity, its own well-defined sense of place, by deriving a mythical significance from the round of daily events that it meticulously records, the quotidian reality of those events still exerts its influence on the poetry. From *Door Into the Dark,* "A Lough Neagh Sequence" collects the legends of the fishermen who live on the lough. The poem, because of its length and ambition, has received the most serious critical attention of any poem from the first two books, and John Wilson Foster has helpfully located some of the immediate sources of the poem. One of them is a nineteenth-century ichthyological work:

> Latter-day scientific sources of "A Lough Neagh Sequence" are un-known, and do not matter, but we do know of one 19th-century source. The sequence was published separately by the Phoenix Pamphlet Poets Press (Manchester, 1969) and had as epigraphs two quotations from *The Fishes of Great Britain and Ireland,* 2 vols. (London, 1880–84), by Francis Day. Scientific in intent, Day's book nonetheless discusses the superstitions surrounding the eel throughout history, perhaps in an attempt to bridge the sizeable gaps in contemporary biology of the eel.[16]

As Foster shows, this scientific knowledge provides the basis for Heaney's budding mythopoeic energies. The fascinating history of the eel's life cycle—it involves mysterious driftings from the Sargasso Sea across the Atlantic to Ireland—is compared to the laborious lives of the eel fishermen. Their labors, however, are given contexts, are given meaning in the poem by the superstitions and customs that attend them. The poem, in fact, is archaeological in its attempt to unearth and record these customs, and when that has been accomplished, a sizable part of the poem's intention has been fulfilled. Just as the oldest English pastorals often reorganized the classical myths, presenting them in contemporary contexts, so Heaney's poem records the local legends of these fishermen. Here is a world of mythopoeia and ichthyology, of poetic fiction and empirical fact, and their conjunction creates the sense of cultural integrity that arises from the involved network of morals, mores, and manners that bind a community together.

Much can be said—and has been said—about the specific details of the myth that Heaney forges here, but beyond that consideration lies the matter of pastoral form, of how the poem, when read in light of its sources, incorporates the biological world within its purview, thus accommodating the pastoral's need for factual authenticity. The memorialization of a community requires an eye for the memorial detail, the significant fact that seems at once local in its reference, yet transcendent in its implication; and just as nostalgia, love, and labor represent for Clare and Heaney important elements of their pastoral, they share also an ability to reconcile dramatically the need to record the daily activities of their community with the aesthetic demands made by their poems. Although one purpose of the lough sequence has been to recover the mythical structures, the ordering principles that shape the fishermen's lives, another purpose has been to account for the hooks, boats, filaments, and barrels that continually intrude on the idealizing powers of myth, reasserting the primacy of tangible things. This particular tension between vision and reality has always characterized pastoral writing, even in Virgil's depiction of a sumptuous Italian countryside that was also a land of exile and homelessness. In section seven, the last and clearly transcendent section, Heaney combines a childhood fear of drowning from lice entwined in his hair with the grim spectacle of seeing eels in a field:

> Unless his hair was fine-combed
> The lice, they said, would gang up
> Into a mealy rope
> And drag him, small, dirty, doomed
>
> Down to the water. He was
> Cautious then in riverbank
> Fields. Thick as a birch trunk
> That cable flexed in the grass
>
> Every time the wind passed. Years
> Later in the same fields
> He stood at night when eels
> Moved through the grass like hatched fears
>
> Towards the water. To stand
> In one place as the field flowed
> Past, a jellied road,
> To watch the eels crossing land

55

Re-wound his world's live girdle.
Phosphorescent, sinewed slime
Continued at his feet. Time
Confirmed the horrid cable.

Such poetry requires a naturalist's curiosity articulated with a my-thographer's sense of proportion and implication. For all pastoral writ-ers, the cycles of the natural world leap from the mundane to the metaphoric, and in the following passage from one of Clare's journals, the naturalist's curiosity is fired by the local legend concerning the birth of eels:

> . . . it has been asserted that eels fall with the rain in ponds it has been so asserted because they did not know how to account for it in any other way—once when I was a young man on staying late at a feast I cross[d] a meadow about midnight and saw to my supprise quantitys of small nimble things emigrating across it a long way from any water I thought at first they were snakes but I found on a closer observation that the[y] were young eels making for a large pond call[d] the Islet pool which they journeyd to with as much knowledge as if they were acquainted with their way I thought this a wonderful discovery then but I have since observd the same thing in larger eels going from one pond to another in the day time and I caught two very large ones in the act of emigrating[17]

In one sense, Clare's observations are debunking ones, dispelling the old accounts of an eel's gestation and birth, but in another, less clinical way, Clare answers Johnson's plea for authenticity. This capacity to erect a mythical apparatus, a symbolic structure that broadens the scope of the poetry and gives it a wider significance while still nurturing a factual, often antimythical perspective, derives ultimately from the first of the *Eclogues* where Meliboeus, wandering through the sumptuous Italian countryside, is an authentic political exile.

Authenticity need not always sober the reader. For Clare and Heaney, another aspect of this local vision derives much of its strength from a keenly developed domestic sensibility, a sensibility alert to the comings and goings in the kitchen, around the fireside, and behind the barn. Churning butter at Mossbawn, Heaney's childhood farm, provided the poet with an opportunity to capture the Northern Irish cadence, to bestow legitimacy on an activity and a community that had previously eluded modern poetry. The first two collections contain poems descriptive of the backyard barn, berries in the byre, wells, an unlicensed bull, a blacksmith's forge, a thatcher, a frozen pump, and bags of seed—all of the animals, foods, and occupations associated with the maintenance of a home in the country. Clare's list would be no less exhaustive. But the most elucidating parallel between their various domesticities concerns their response to marriage. Both wrote poems that specifically address the subject of their recent unions, and they chose a remarkably similar and distinctive set of images to do so. Clare was married on March 16, 1820, and the poem that arose from the occasion was entitled "Proposals for Building a Cottage":

> Beside a runnel build my shed
> Wi' stubbles coverd oer
> Let broad oaks oer its chimley spread
> And grass plats grace the door
>
> The door may open wi a string
> So that it closes tight
> And locks too woud be wanted things
> To keep out thieves at night
>
> A little garden not too fine
> Inclosed with painted pails
> And wood bines round the cot to twine
> Pind to the wall wi nails
>
> Let hazels grow and spindling sedge
> Bent bowering over head
> Dig old mans bear from woodland hedge
> To twine a summer shade
>
> Beside the threshold sods provide
> And build a summer seat
> Plant sweet briar bushes by its side
> And flowers that smelleth sweet
>
> I love the sparrows way to watch
> Upon the cotters sheds
> So here and there pull out the thatch
> As they may hid[e] their heads

And as the sweeping swallows stop
Their flights along the green
Leave holes within the chimney top
To paste their nest between

Stick shelves and cupboards round the hut
In all the holes and nooks
Nor in the corner fail to put
A cubboard for the books

Along the floor some sand I['] ll sift
To make it fit to live in
And the I['] ll thank ye for the gift
As somthing worth the giving

Heaney's version of this architectural metaphor appears in "Poem,"
dedicated to Marie, his wife, and included in his first book, *Death of a
Naturalist:*

Love, I shall perfect for you the child
Who diligently potters in my brain
Digging with heavy spade till sods were piled
Or puddling through muck in a deep drain.

Yearly I would sow my yard-long garden.
I'd strip a layer of sods to build the wall
That was to exclude sow and pecking hen.
Yearly, admitting these, the sods would fall.

Or in the sucking clabber I would splash
Delightedly and dam the flowing drain
But always my bastions of clay and mush
Would burst before the rising autumn rain.

Love, you shall perfect for me this child
Whose small imperfect limits would keep breaking:
Within new limits now, arrange the world
Within our walls, within our golden ring.

Both Clare and Heaney delight here in measurement, the sobering
science of fixing "new limits," as Heaney has it, or planting a garden "in-
closed wi painted pails," as Clare has it. Clare's sense of perfection

concerns his ideal house, and Heaney's his fondly recalled childhood. Tape measures and building plans come to mind when first confronting the title of Clare's poem, "Proposals for Building a Cottage," and Heaney's portrayal of his childhood relies on both words and phrases that yearn for an architectural precision: "build a wall," "exclude," "admitting these," "dam the . . . drain," "bastions," and "limits." If Heaney's subject is more explicitly that of marriage and its possibilities and Clare's more that of housing and landscaping, they both nonetheless share a concern for the family, the community—in this case—of two. Even among the welter of the antipastoralists, the poetry retained its capacity for idealizing, for dreaming of an earthly Eden, and when Heaney begins by claiming that he will "perfect" the mud-caked child who "potters in [his] brain," he renews an essential feature of the tradition. Both poets speak of a "garden" and "sods," and this rural imagery, when combined with the confrontational aspects of the poem hinted at by the walls, locks, thieves, and dams, provides yet another example of the pastoral vision as an essentially opposing one. The literary strategies of both poems seem naturally, or perhaps more accurately, natively, derived from the rural culture that provided the poets with their images and ideas; and although they belong to that species of poems known as "occasional," the occasion here—marital love—leads to the threshold of the bridal chamber. The essential spirit of these two poems finds its forebear in the epithalamium, one of the signal forms of pastoral writing, and its celebration of the marriage vow, blending rural imagery with the marital ritual, provides each poet with another means of celebrating one of the rites of his community. Celebration, an art that wilted at Crabbe's touch, was resuscitated by Clare and thrives in Heaney's version of pastoral.

Clare and Heaney, then, share first and foremost a devotion to their rural communities, and this devotion resulted in the development of poetic styles that would both celebrate yet faithfully render the particular situations of those communities in the social and political hierarchy. Yet coincidence carries no argumentative weight; few poets have failed to write, at some time in their career, about the peculiar persuasions of the countryside. Whether the countryside is seen in the daisy or the daisy is seen in the countryside distinguishes perhaps the mystical from the mysterious, but neither the daisy's petal nor the woodland vista can alone be counted as the defining element of pastoral literature. Although panoramas and petals flourish in the poetry of Clare and Heaney, they flourish in specific, assertively described localities. The particularized descriptions of the poetry are intended not only to establish the authenticity that has been one of the main concerns of the latter-day pastoral, but also, by cultivating such an authenticity, to dramatize the distinguishing elements of their own communities. Although Clare was never beleaguered by doubts of his Englishness, his nationhood, as Heaney has been denied his Irishry, Clare's and Heaney's work both confront the problem of infiltrating a literary hierarchy unsympathetic to the values that would most distinguish a true and sympathetic portrayal of their own subcultures. And their literary strategies, deploying certain features of the pastoral tradition, reflect the several similarities of their enterprises.

Such dramatizations of communities, of the beliefs and principles that weld communities together and constitute political entities, draw on a vigorous literary tradition in Ireland. In fact, much of the country's history, from Henry II's successful campaign in the twelfth century to Margaret Thatcher's junkets to Dublin, can be seen as a series of repeated, often repetitive, attempts by one community to establish superiority over—often masquerading as parity with—another community. Through a long and complex history of assault, repulsion, and amalgamation, both the Irish Free State and Northern Ireland have come implicitly to envision political action as the careful curator of the varied cultural concerns that distinguish each community. And just as these cultural allegiances are finely shaded into unbreachable differences, so the political solutions offered by various groups, parties, assemblies, and armies seem unalterably at odds with one another. Yet perhaps it is not too simplistic to observe that the labels most often and most deceptively used to distinguish the two divisions of the island—Catholic and Protestant—both speak of a concern for the definition of their country, a problem that ultimately faces all partitioned communities.

To chart and explain the gradual evolution of this definition provides historians with their defining labor. It should come as no surprise to the student of Irish history that, because the cultural foundations of the country have so clearly helped to determine the country's political apparatus, the literary artists of Ireland, both in the Free State and the six counties, appear continually in discussions of Ireland's history. Perhaps Kavanagh's cynical assessment of the Irish Literary Revival corrected the extravagant dreams that its principal writers had of the native Irishry, but even if Synge's Aran Islands or Yeats's peasants *were* literary lies partly bred and encouraged by the English, we must, if we are fully to appreciate Heaney's poetry, examine its polemical aspects. Richard Fallis is atrociously accurate when he calls Kavanagh, making his way through Dublin during the 1930s, a "professional bumpkin";[18] and like Kavanagh's cultivated parochialism, Heaney's "rurallity," his version of Ireland's fallowed pastures, is part and parcel of his urbanity, his vision of the legislative halls that surround those pastures. The subject of political poetry arises here, and pastoral writing, with its penchant for allegory, has traditionally been pressed into political service.

But Heaney's poetry resists the simplifications of the word "political," a word often encountered in discussions of his work. Too often, readers have taken the term in its narrowest, most constricting sense, and examples of these cases speak louder than discussions of these cases. In an interview with *Ploughshares,* Heaney was asked if it were possible for a poet to live in Belfast. The year is 1979, seven years after Heaney left the North and moved to the Republic:

> Of course it's possible for a poet to live in Belfast still, if he chooses to do so. . . . I left in 1972 not really out of any rejection of Belfast but because . . . I had the name for being a poet, but I was also discovering myself being interviewed, as more or less, a spokesman for the Catholic minority during this early stage of the troubles. I found the whole question of what was the status of art within my own life and the question of what is an artist to do in a political situation very urgent matters.

The interviewer wants to know if the move to the Republic had occasioned a sense of guilt:

> Well, I suppose the violence and the crisis in the public domain and the demand that was made on every writer heightened and made more urgent a lot of questions I had been thinking of for myself. . . . Undoubtedly I was aware of a political dimension to the move to the south of the border, and it was viewed, I think, with regret by some, and with a sense of almost betrayal by others. That was because a situation like that in the north of Ireland generates a great energy and group loyalty, and it generates a defensiveness about its own verities. Some people felt rejected by my leaving but it wasn't a matter of me rejecting anyone but of my own growth. . . . I was quite content in a way to accept and undergo that political dimension because I had never considered myself British. . . . I had no doubt about the rightness of the move itself but I was bothered by some of its consequences, such as seeming to break ranks with my friends there.[19]

Heaney's answers reveal a clear emphasis on nourishing the writer's occupation, on making decisions—practical decisions—that will guard the various sources of that nourishment. But his concern for his community has continued unabated, and although he has studiously avoided the cramping noise of political rhetoric, he has remained alert to the nuances of his own position in the Anglo-Irish community.

Heaney's interest in the nature of political writing has developed over the years, gradually expanding to include the literature from Eastern Bloc countries. In his essay, "The Impact of Translation," he responds to a poem by Milosz: "It counted for much that this poem was written by somebody who resisted the Nazi occupation of Poland and broke from the ranks of the People's Republic after the war and paid for the principle and pain of all that with a lifetime of exile and self-scrutiny." The essay confesses a mitigated envy for writers of the Soviet Union and the Warsaw Pact countries "whose poetry . . . testifies thereby to the continuing efficacy of poetry itself as a necessary and redemptive mode of being human." Heaney's abiding interest in these Eastern Bloc poets derives from their "modern martyrology, a record of courage and sacrifice which elicits our unstinted admiration." But he is concerned with English poetry also, and he warily suggests that "poets in English sense the locus of poetic greatness shifting away from their language."[20] An unsympathetic reader might accuse Heaney of assuming that great admirable subjects yield great admirable poems; his enthusiasm for these poems often seems unbridled, even undiscriminating.

But Heaney is aware, as the interview indicated, of what Eliot referred to as the "social function of poetry," a phrase whose generous connotations situate the poet in the larger context of society. Eliot, ever the rear-guard anglophile, seems an odd example to cite when discussing Heaney's political motivations, but Eliot had at one time loomed large in Heaney's conception of modern literature. And however loyal were the colors of Eliot's canon, his engulfing literary sensibilities led him to address the fundamental questions that must inform any discussion of political literature. Eliot's brilliance as a polemicist lay in his ability to concoct the reasonable generality, and many of his critical formulations have become the slogans of an age. Although sloganeering sacrifices conceptual subtlety for emotional simplicity, Eliot's opinions on the political aspects of poetry deserve careful attention because they represent the opinions of a man for whom English culture was initially a distant if not foreign one. The many problems associated with defining a national culture—a subject which has obviously engaged Heaney— form the nucleus of Eliot's poetry and prose, and one essay in particular neatly categorizes the essential perspectives that must order a discussion of the broader cultural and political aspects of Heaney's work.

In his address, "The Social Function of Poetry," Eliot succinctly outlined his thoughts on the place of poetry in society, particularly the society of the English-speaking world. The most revealing insight is the one most bluntly given: "We may say that the duty of the poet, as poet, is only indirectly to his people: his direct duty is to his *language,* first to preserve, and second to extend and improve." Eliot's anglophilia often resulted—shrewdly—in a literally insular linguistics, and this paper, delivered in 1943, came late in Eliot's spiritual development. But his conception of a poet's "duty" to the language is an embracing and thoroughly benevolent one:

> So far I have only suggested the final point to which I think the influence of poetry may be said to extend; and that can be put best by the assertion that, in the long run, it makes a difference to the speech, to the sensibility, to the lives of all the members of a society, to all the members of the community, to the whole people, whether they read and enjoy poetry or not. . . . And this is what I mean by the social function of poetry in its largest sense: that it does, in proportion to its excellence and vigour, affect the speech and the sensibility of the whole nation.[21]

Although part of Eliot's concern in this essay is inherently literary—"It is . . . through the living authors that the dead remain alive"—his literary concerns often seem to relish a kind of national privacy—"Poetry is a constant reminder of all the things that can only be said in one language, and are untranslatable." English poetry, in Eliot's terms, embodies an intangible Englishness, and as a result, represents the quintessence of the English "community." Along with Pound, Eliot was one of the century's fervent advocates of translation, and he was also one of the keenest judges of the risks, losses, and benefits that attend the translator. The impossibility of rendering a translation thoroughly faithful to its original language sharpens our appreciation of the immense possibilities that lie in the poetry residing in our mother tongue.

In the same essay, Eliot had briefly addressed the problem of political poetry; the brevity of his address, it seems, stems from the conceptual poverty of his subject:

> The whole question of the relation of countries of different language but related culture, within the ambit of Europe, is therefore one into

which we are led, perhaps unexpectedly, by inquiring into the social function of poetry. I certainly do not intend to pass from this point into purely political questions; but I could wish that those who are concerned with political questions would more often cross the frontier into these which I have been considering. For these give the spiritual aspect of problems the material aspect of which is the concern of politics.[22]

Is there a note of condescension in Eliot's wish, a priestly insistence that our political writers concern themselves with the "spiritual aspect" of these broad cultural problems? Perhaps so. But what seems condescension to the condescended will seem spiritual philanthropy to the condescenders. Like those of all religious thinkers, Eliot's program—if such a deceptively coherent term accurately describes his complicated spiritual, intellectual, and emotional development—depends on establishing the larger context, the framework that will order and give value to the mundane course of our daily lives. For Eliot, political concerns and, more specifically, political poetry are best understood, most effectively enacted, within the boundaries established by such a context. And for this particular context he reserves the eminent adjective "spiritual."

To arrive at this station of eminence, Eliot "cross[ed] the frontier." Presumably, this is a frontier littered with special interests and interested specialists. Poetry that solely addresses itself to the minutiae of contemporary opinion is a poetry, in Eliot's words, that "may have a transient vogue when the poet is reflecting a popular attitude of the moment." The opposite also holds true. Poetry that raises certain attitudes to a level of notoriety, reflecting unpopular opinions and beliefs, will claim our attention for as long as the issues that breed such unpopularity remain current ones. "Real poetry," Eliot continues, "survives not only a change of popular opinion but the complete extinction of interest in the issues with which the poet was passionately concerned." To the committed Unionist, to the committed Republican, Eliot often seems unaware of passionate concern, and he occasionally provides a good example of Michael Hamburger's observation on Yeats: "Contempt for politics is of course a characteristic Conservative stance."[23]

The wide range of questions implied and unexamined—what is, then, "real poetry"?—by Eliot's essay makes it both a frustrating and suggestive piece of work. On one hand, the essay is a fervent defense of poetry, and it occasionally achieves a rhetorical, Whitmanesque tone, arguing that poetry exists for the "whole of the people." On the other hand, Eliot remains suspicious of such undiscriminating benevolence; one of the twentieth century's characteristic problems, he claims, is its "inability to *feel* towards God and man. . . ." And when these religious *feelings* disappear, the poetry becomes impoverished by their absence. Eliot ends his essay with wry sarcasm: "It is equally possible that the feeling for poetry, and the feelings which are the material of poetry, may disappear everywhere: which might perhaps help to facilitate that unification of the world which some people consider desirable for its own sake."[24] Poetry, as Eliot warned earlier, resides most powerfully in the original language where it nervously exhibits the intonations of the culture that produced it. But these intonations, these syntactic noises, are safely stored within the boundaries of the language. Translation, at best, affords artful equivalences. So when Eliot speaks of "the whole of the people," he is, in one sense, thinking of the whole of the people who speak English, or Italian, or French; and the "unification of the world" will come about when the proper "feeling" for poetry is lost, a clear and cynically rendered notion that, in Eliot's terms, poetry realizes those feelings unique to each culture.

But unique feelings are, occasionally, divisive ones, insisting, as they must, on their uniqueness. Taken to extremes, the concept of a national, untranslatable "feeling" leads to the dream of a national, untranslatable sovereignty, and, at this point, poetry becomes little more than eloquent sloganeering. To Eliot such sloganeering was an abomination. That he was concerned to reconcile, in his terms, poetry's local, political vision with its universal, spiritual one is clearly indicated by the elaborate imprecisions of his essay. As Eliot's career progresses, it becomes increasingly helpful to view him as a religious poet and to view his essays, plays, and poetry as literary explorations of his subject. Seen within this context, the imprecisions of his essay are not as imprecise as they are mysterious—his stylistic devices ultimately derive their tone from the Christian mysteries that define his faith.

For Eliot, then, the political aspects of poetry were judged and evaluated within a larger context, the spiritual context readily available to those who would "cross the frontier." Heaney too has written on the political aspects of his own poetry, and because the political problems of Heaney's Ireland stand in antithetical relation to those of Eliot's England, his thoughts on the subject develop many of the concerns Eliot passionately subordinated. Delivered in October 1974 to the Royal Society of Literature and later included in his collection of essays entitled *Preoccupations* (1980), "Feeling Into Words" represents Heaney's most candid and concise assessment of political poetry. Referring to the summer of 1969, a watershed for the civil rights movement in Northern Ireland, Heaney explains how and why his verse suddenly shifted its focus. The entire passage merits quotation because it chronicles the broadening vision that Eliot, from an entirely different perspective, cultivated whenever he spoke of poetry's function in society:

> From that moment the problems of poetry moved from being simply a matter of achieving the satisfactory verbal icon to being a search for images and symbols adequate to our predicament. I do not mean liberal lamentation that citizens should feel compelled to murder one another or deploy their different military arms over the matter of nomenclatures such as British or Irish. I do not mean public celebrations or execrations of resistance or atrocity. . . . I mean that I felt it imperative to discover a field of force in which, without abandoning fidelity to the processes and experience of poetry as I have outlined them, it would be possible to encompass the perspectives of a humane reason and at the same time to grant the religious intensity of the violence its deplorable authenticity and complexity.[25]

As was the case in Eliot's essay, Heaney's terminology resists specificity. The description of the poem as a "verbal icon" scolds the New Critics for the narrow aestheticism they promulgated, and Heaney's attempt to find methods and images "adequate to [the] predicament" in Northern Ireland argues for a measure of social responsibility. But Heaney avoids offering a precise definition of "adequate." Instead his general guidelines are broadly descriptive of his verse, and perhaps that is the point. A tendency to envision simultaneously, perhaps even to reconcile urgently, the grace of reason and the necessity of violence, and to do so by granting the latter its "deplorable authenticity," represents one of pastoral's essential features—the dramatic representation of mutually subversive images, ideas, and themes within an idealized rural landscape. These representations must occur within certain contexts and must fulfill certain expectations if they are to qualify as pastoral. For Eliot, political poetry, or even political issues, seemed a way station between the "hither and the farther shore," as he has it in *The Dry Salvages;* but for Heaney, the question of nationhood and racial identity has provided one of the emotional matrices that nourish his verse. As a result, Heaney's early work resembles a militarized pastoral, one that draws both on the ameliorating nostalgia traditionally associated with the genre and on the various imageries and dictions associated with war or political unrest.

As Blake Morrison has shown, the earliest reviews of Heaney's first two books classified them as examples of "post-1945 nature poetry—an imprecisely defined genre, but one presided over by Ted Hughes and reputed to be in opposition to 'idealized' Georgian treatments of nature. . . ." And these classifications are not as skewed as Morrison's own observation requires them to be: "the most striking feature of Seamus Heaney's first two books . . . is their mediation between silence and speech."[26] Both approaches to the poetry yield fruitful readings, one correctly emphasizing obvious literary debts to Hughes's language and imagery, the other discovering an important theme that extends throughout Heaney's verse and culminates in the aptly titled lyric from *North,* "Whatever You Say Say Nothing."

The first collection, *Death of a Naturalist,* abounds in graphically rendered rural images, and in this sense, they reflect most immediately the methods of Hughes's *Lupercal* (1960). Gathered in that widely influential volume are foxes, stoats, tomcats, hawks, bulls, pigs, crabs, otters, thrushes, pike, bullfrogs, and goats. Heaney's bestiary, though it includes many of the same animals, memorializes the memory that preserves them. As a result, his descriptions are often enthusiastic portrayals of an era that seems securely removed from the problems of Northern Ireland. In "Digging," Heaney comes to a full stop, as if amazed by his father's dexterity, punctuating the narrative with an interjection: "My God, the old man could handle a spade," he writes after carefully describing his father at work in his garden. Such eager energy pervades much of the poetry, and in its eagerness to record the frogs, barns, blackberries, churns, kittens, plows, and potatoes that crowded his boyhood, the poetry seems, broadly, inaccurately, and nostalgically speaking, pastoral.

In the same year that *Death of a Naturalist* appeared, however, Heaney wrote an article for *The New Statesman* entitled "Out of London: Ulster's Troubles." He chose not to include it in *Preoccupations.* The essay discusses the possibilities of carrying on the writer's life in Belfast of the late 60s, but it begins by describing the essential spirit of the city:

Although it is the official capital of the partitioned state of Northern Ireland and although its citizens regard themselves definitely as "townies," it is impossible to forget that Belfast is essentially a country town. . . . The natural encroaches on the urban in all sorts of ways.

> Several of the main buildings and High Street, one of the main thor-
> oughfares, are built over what is now an underground river that in the
> early days flowed down the centre of High Street to the docks. Names
> like Falls Road and Malone Road (preserves of the Nationalist mass
> and the bourgeois ascendancy respectively) are Anglicised forms of
> Gaelic names, indicative of former *pastoral* conditions—"the road of
> the hedges," "the plain of the lambs." (emphasis mine)[27]

The Falls Road, a Catholic enclave since the reign of Queen Elizabeth I,
originally comprised the area immediately beyond the gates of the city.
Barred from living in Belfast, the native population of the island used the
path through the scrublands to the mountains as an escape route during
times of civil unrest. The area, now a part of the city, has become synony-
mous with the nationalist movement, and it is important to note that
Heaney invokes the "pastoral" etymology of the word to characterize the
Road's presiding spirit. Conjuring up "the road of the hedges," an an-
cient Celtic stronghold, Heaney implicitly acknowledges that strain of re-
sistance which has long been a distinguishing feature of pastoral poetry.

Following this introduction, the essay provides an analysis of life in
Belfast both powerful in its sympathies and balanced in its eventual as-
sessments. The perspective is that of a writer, but a writer concerned, or
simply frightened, by the "stabbings, shootings and bomb-throwings."
In 1966, Heaney's intuitions are darkly prophetic: "A month ago it was
still possible to say "hooliganism," but with the shooting down of three
youths on Sunday and the death of one of them nobody can ignore the
threat to public safety."[28] In less than three years, another Sunday in
January would receive the attributive title "Bloody" when thirteen civil
rights demonstrators were shot and killed in Derry, Northern Ireland. It is
important for American readers to understand how conspicuously politi-
cal turmoil and violence shaped Heaney's sense of community during the
composition of the early work. His verse, in one aspect, subtly records
that violence and turmoil, and provides a good example of the many
ways in which poetry responds to political issues without sacrificing its
aesthetic integrity.

How then in Eliot's terms, does Heaney understand the social func-
tion of poetry? And having come to such an understanding, how does he
bring this understanding to bear on the work at hand, the work that he
hoped was "adequate to our predicament"? The article in *The New
Statesman,* published in July, appeared two months after Faber brought
out *Death of a Naturalist.* And the poems often seem to embody this

68

violence with their diction alone. A catalog of these poems would be unnecessarily laborious, a list of the relevant words and phrases appearing throughout the collection specifically helpful: *gun, armoury, grenade, bridgehead, pottery bombs, sentry, reconaissance, parachutists, reveille, attacking, breaking* . . . *ranks, flotilla, hunting, beached, squadrons, fuselage, wings, tail-fan, rudder, depth-charge, gun-barrel, tracer-bullet, volley, cowling, barrage, re-enter* . . . *the port, command,* and once more, *grenade.* The large majority of these are included in passages given over entirely to the description of country life.

These aggressive renditions of a Catholic boyhood in rural Northern Ireland stand at the center of Heaney's early version of pastoral. In *The New Statesman,* Heaney had wondered how living in Belfast might affect a writer's work, and he had offered two opinions, imagining that it "might induce a sense of claustrophobia and a desire to escape." But he added that Belfast might "concentrate a man's energies on the immediate dramatic complex of tension and intrigue." Finally, with a note of casual condescension, he enjoined: "Of course the uncommitted and the skeptical tend to leave, or to be elbowed out."[29] Six years later, in 1972, Heaney left Belfast and moved to the Republic; both his critics and his apologists found an opportunity for explaining their ideas on the subject of political allegiance. But the record of those allegiances lies in the poetry written while Heaney was living in Belfast, the poems that often fall under the aegis of twentieth-century pastoral. Through a painstaking attention to the individual features of his community—its animals, its people, its landscapes—Heaney has created a version of rural Catholic Ireland that cherishes its own ideals without eroding those of the surrounding English community. His version is aggressively rendered but respectfully submitted, and when ensconced in the often nostalgically devised rural scenes of the early work, this combination of aggression and respect, of violent energy and conservative restraint, creates the aesthetic tensions associated with pastoral writing.

But these tensions have been largely structural in nature. The concern for authenticity evident in Johnson's criticisms of "Lycidas" became the bellwether for many of the later writers of the antipastoral tradition. Clare, a fortunate compromise, avoided the extremes of Crabbe's strident revisionism, yet cultivated an adoring eye for realism, and this happy conjunction provided Heaney with a model for his own shrewd appraisals of the rural community in Northern Ireland, an appraisal that allowed him to develop a poetry that would grant the violence of Northern Ireland its "deplorable authenticity." In this context, authenticity

69

results in a moving portrayal of country life based on a diction of violence and resistance, and this tension between the lovingly described landscape and the aggressive terminology of its description provides his early verse with its essential link to one of pastoral poetry's most important structural elements. When used to describe twentieth-century literature, however, the term pastoral most often refers to theme and subject matter, and the genre has traditionally been employed to examine several recurring ideas or concerns. Heaney's later work abandons these more obvious techniques of composition, a formal concern, and develops several essentially pastoral ideas, a thematic concern.

Rocks, Caves, Lakes, Fens,
Bogs, Dens, and Shades of Death:
The Radical Pastoral
of *Wintering Out* and *North*

Nostalgia is a surreptitious sentiment, and when it provides the emotional order for a poem, it does so in subtle and deceptive ways. Often, for example, Virgil's "Eclogue 1"—a good story about dispossession and political favor—is moving because it is, simply, a good story. How, the reader wonders, has Tityrus managed to retain his land while Meliboeus is being driven from *his* land? Political history supplies factual answers, none of which satisfy the appetite for gossip—what, specifically, did Tityrus *do* for Augustus that allowed him to retain his land? Or perhaps, what had Meliboeus refused or failed to do, what had he avoided doing that Tityrus had done eagerly, regretfully, or unknowingly? The variations on this theme of political intrigue are as numerous as the connotations of the words Virgil deftly used to describe it, and interpreters of the poem have resolutely recognized the bewildering array of seductions, bribes, and favors that might possibly sharpen the mellifluous tones of the Latin verse. Laurence Lerner, however, recognizes the poem's definitive burden, the one often missed by readers mired in the titillating scandal of it all: "Loss of home, and the sadness of Meliboeus at being driven out: this Eclogue is drenched in nostalgia."[1]

So the foreground of the poem, the domineering details of the intrigue, are played out against the nurturing background of nostalgia.

Lerner continues by building a convincing case for the ubiquity of nostalgia in pastoral writing, and the individual elements of Heaney's pastoral myth continually recall the important implications of Lerner's lesson. Nostalgia alone, although an essential element of much pastoral writing, cannot raise a work of drudgery to the ranks of inspired literature. Nor does the pastoral jealously restrict the purview of nostalgia. Writers who look wistfully over their shoulders toward a better time assume the risks of recollection, and a bovine complacency is not the worst of the maladies that afflicts the dreaming bard. Nostalgia, when it becomes an indulgence, anesthetizes the memory, encouraging the irresponsible assessments of the past that render judgments on the present incredible.

Heaney's poetry deals gingerly with the notions of history and judgment. Unafraid of grappling with the political issues that currently divide his country, the verse is equally bold as it ransacks his own personal history and the history of his country for the appropriate metaphor, the correct image, "adequate," as he has written, "to our predicament." His predicament, his cultural perspective, is one continually confronted by a long tradition of sectarian violence, and the vision of the past gradually revealed in his verse begins and ends in interrogation, demanding to know whether or not peace and violence represent the two guises of historical progress. If reconstructing the community of his childhood or the genealogy of his race in rural Northern Ireland brings him closer to resolving this issue, then nostalgia has returned to its pastoral context, its nourishing provenance.

The study of racial history often leads the student far afield, engendering comparisons between cultures that would seem to share little in their current state of development. Heaney's discovery—through a book on the subject—of Denmark's bog people has become the stuff of literary trivia in the late twentieth century. *The Bog People,* written by P. V. Glob and first published in 1969, contained photographs of men and women whose bodies had been remarkably preserved by the tanning agents present in the bogs where they had lain for almost two thousand years. Many of those found had clearly been the victims of a ritual sacrifice. These Norsemen first invaded Ireland during the eighth century, and Heaney began to cultivate the obvious parallels between their adventuresome and violent culture and the one that now divides contemporary Ireland. The Tollund Man, for example, was discovered in the spring of

1950. He was lying in the Tollund Fen in Bjaeldskov Dale, and he is now on display in the Silkeborg Museum, six miles from the fen; Heaney's description of the man reveals a genealogical sympathy:

> The Tollund Man seemed like an ancestor almost, one of my old uncles, one of those moustached archaic faces you used to meet all over the Irish countryside. I just felt very close to this. And the sacrificial element, the territorial religious element, the whole mythological field surrounding these images was very potent. So I tried, not explicitly, to make a connection between the sacrificial, religious element in the violence of contemporary Ireland and this terrible religious thing in *The Bog People*.[2]

Religious ritual, social hierarchy, nutrition, village organization— Glob's book offers an engrossing account of an Iron Age culture. "Bogland," the final poem of *Door Into the Dark,* introduced these seeping, preserving landscapes in Heaney's verse, and "Bog Oak" from the next collection, *Wintering Out,* developed the interest; but "The Tollund Man," which appears in the same volume, was the first poem to investigate the Iron Age culture of Denmark, an investigation that would culminate in the poems of *North.* This was Heaney's fourth full-length collection, and because of its imaginative and ambitious excavations, of both the historical tradition and the racial genealogies that gave birth to his own society, the book has received widespread critical acclaim. Pastoral writing depends on nostalgia to make attractive its vision of the past, and Virgil's old Italy, lovingly depicted, allowed the poet to suffer the slings and arrows of an outrageous emperor. But for Heaney, Denmark's Iron Age provides the dire precedent for the problems of Northern Ireland, and it is hard to overestimate the importance of the poet's discovery that the pastures of his Irish childhood were first tended by a culture whose forefathers practiced ritual murder.

Both visions of the past provide an imaginative compensation for the poet and allow each to view his own society from another distant perspective. Heaney does not long for the countryside of ancient Tollund as Virgil longs for the countryside of pre-Augustan Italy. Heaney's vision ironically reverses the role of traditional pastoral nostalgia because his conjured past, though it leads ultimately to toleration and understanding as all Golden Ages must, participated in sacrificial killing. By revising one of the central conventions of pastoral literature, Heaney has located a historical tradition for the secular martyrdom of the North.

The poems that deal with the bog people do not display the wistful remembrances typically associated with poems given to the backward look, the nostalgic vision. In Virgil's "Eclogue 4," the poet had prophesied the fall of an Iron Age ("ferrea"), a mythological designation; and in Glob's book, the scientist had uncovered the inhabitants of yet another Iron Age, an archaeological designation. This coincidence of the mythical and the archaeological reenacts the confrontation between fact and fiction that distinguished Clare's biological approach to the legends concerning the birth of eels—a structural tension also characteristic of pastoral writing. Virgil's Golden Age and "Eclogue 4" in general quickly became for Christians in the early centuries of the first millennium a declaration of ascendancy; as time passed, Virgil steadily became a Golden Age unto himself, and he was in many ways the tutelary spirit of the Renaissance writer. As Heaney places the Iron Age people of Tollund at the focal point of his backward glance, he transforms the vanquished mythological Iron Age of Virgil's "Eclogue 4" into the grimly verifiable Iron Age of Ireland's distant ancestors. Other subjects organize other poems and fall under the broad rubric of a more traditional pastoral nostalgia. From the etymologist to the solitary wanderer, from the languishing lover to the Nordic historian, Heaney tries on different guises in the poetry, and each of them extends the tradition in various ways.

Two of these guises, both of them nostalgic in essence, warrant discussion because they will play a large role in the evolution of *North*. Many of Heaney's poems from this period derive their inspiration from the study of etymology, and if a traditionally oriented nostalgia is in the work, it lies in his reverential approach to the obscured histories, the distant glories of a single word's development. Such a linguistic nostalgia provides fit accompaniment for the other, more expansive excavations carried out in his poems. Even though a foreboding and tenacious violence resides in Heaney's Iron Age, his ameliorating love for old words, his conserving passion for the verbal relics of his culture, assure that the genealogy unearthed in his poems will remain essentially restorative.

Speaking of nostalgia in general, Lerner provides a useful introduction to another aspect of Heaney's version of pastoral when he remarks that Meliboeus, la Malabaraise, and Hardy had "learnt to sing of what they loved by losing it."[3] Loss tests a multitude of strengths but none so poignantly as the strength of love. Pastoral writers, accustomed to envisioning earthly paradises, are fighting Milton's war in Heaven—the innocent and perfected collide with the ruined and ruinous, but while the angelic hosts collect their spoils, pastoral innocence is normally violated. Milton's angels prevail because they must prevail; no such inevitability attends the struggle between good and evil in pastoral writing, and therein lies its complexity, its ability to offer the poet a vast array of metaphors for violation, running the gamut from sexual love to political suppression.

Both the lost word, which etymology recovers, and the lost love, which the poet's erotic imagination recovers, form a clearly related pair of interests in Heaney's version of pastoral. Language and eroticism, for example, are deftly entwined in contexts that evoke pastoral situations. "Ocean's Love to Ireland," included in *North,* refers to Ralegh's poem for Queen Elizabeth, "The Ocean's Love to Cynthia," but in Heaney's version, Ralegh, who is speaking his native dialect, plunders an Irish maid whose naive innocence is unquestionable. No satyrs dance here, but the overriding impression of innocence, the image of the babe-in-the-woods, suggests that Hibernia, like Arcadia of the pastoral tradition, is being pillaged and that its infectious charms will soon be attainable only through the grace of nostalgia:

> Speaking broad Devonshire,
> Ralegh has backed the maid to a tree
> As Ireland is backed to England
>
> And drives inland
> Till all her strands are breathless:
> "Sweesir, Swatter! Sweesir, Swatter!"
>
> He is water, he is ocean, lifting
> Her farthingale like a scarf of weed lifting
> In the front of a wave.

In his introductory book on Heaney, Blake Morrison quotes the passage in John Aubrey's *Brief Lives* that clarifies the history behind the poem. Speaking of Ralegh, Aubrey had written:

> He loved a wench well; and one time getting up one of the Mayds of Honour up against a tree in a Wood ('twas his first Lady) who seemed at first boarding to be something fearfull of her Honour, and modest, she cryed, sweet sir Walter, what doe you me ask; Will you undoe me?

Nay, sweet Sir Walter! Sweet Sir Walter! Sir Walter! At last as the
danger and the pleasure at the same time grew higher, she cryed in the
extasey, Swisser, Swatter, Swisser, Swatter.

Morrison continues by arguing that "Ralegh's 'broad Devonshire' (the
phrase is again Aubrey's) overcom[es] the 'Irish' of the ruined maid."[4]
But the word "overcome," although delightful in its sexual punning,
seems too strong; persistence is an Irish virtue nowhere more prevalent
than in the survival of Gaelic, and even though its future seems question-
able at this stage of the poem, the maid, along with her Irish, "fades" but
never disappears:

> The ruined maid complains in Irish,
> Ocean has scattered her dream of fleets,
> The Spanish prince has spilled his gold
>
> And failed her. Iambic drums
> Of English beat the woods where her poets
> Sink like Onan. Rush-light, mushroom-flesh,
>
> She fades from their somnolent clasp
> Into ringlet-breath and dew,
> The ground possessed and repossessed.

The pendular swing of possession and repossession recalls the
countless struggles between the Irish people and the various conquerors
that set sail from English shores. But the linguistic analogy, which
Heaney emphasizes, provides the shrewder commentary on the pecu-
liarly pastoral conjunction of nationality, physical love, and language.
John Braidwood, in an anthology of essays dedicated to tracing the
history of the English language in Ireland, analyzes the relation between
Elizabethan and Ulster English. He cites several reasons that would
account for the survival of a Shakespearean English in Northern Ireland,
a stronghold not only for Royalist politics, but for the Queen's English as
well:

Irish enthusiasts, on both sides of the border, have long appropriated
the dialectalisms—and, to their credit, even the vulgarisms—to their
own glory in proclaiming that pure Elizabethan English is still to be
heard in whatever English-settled region of Ireland the enthusiast

happens to come from. Dr. St. John Ervine advised his readers to go to Ulster if they wanted to hear English spoken as it was in Shakespeare's day. . . .[5]

Heaney's etymological nostalgia, his fondness for the ecstatic contractions found in the phrases "sweesir" and "swatter" initiates a light-hearted origin myth for the legacy of suppression that survives in Northern Ireland. The Irish maid backed against the tree, indicates that her spoiled innocence is a *fait accompli,* that pastoral dreams, hopeful though they may be, arise from a plundered world. This important paradox of the genre allows Heaney to cultivate simultaneously the nostalgic perspective of old Hibernia and the politically realistic one of a conquered island.

In "Traditions," a poem from *Wintering Out,* Heaney admits that "We are to be proud/Of our Elizabethan English," but the assertive tone of the declaration makes the sentiment seem forced, especially when the poem had begun by stating succinctly that "Our guttural muse/Was bulled long ago/By the alliterative tradition. . . ." When Ralegh pinned the Irish maid to the tree, he left her with more than his child. The couple represents for Heaney a fusion of the guttural and the alliterative; significantly, the product of that union, the child, is never mentioned by Aubrey or Heaney, and as the child must have grown up a bastard, so Heaney's version of English occasionally expresses concern about its proper parentage. Yet the poems of *Wintering Out* and *North* attempt to discover the parentage, both in its linguistic and historical dimensions. Because the poetry continually looks to the past to dramatize and understand the culture of contemporary Ireland, and because it looks to a past that is simple, even primitive, in its orientation, the poetry remains closely aligned with the fundamental nostalgia associated with the pastoral tradition.

But Heaney's mythical apparatus did not arrive fully developed, as if by divine fiat, and a brief glance at an earlier poem shows that Heaney's imaginative sympathies have long been directed toward the preserving landscape, the landscape that magically provides contemporary Ireland with the physical evidence of its cultural tradition. In the *Ploughshares* interview, Heaney confessed to having been angered by a "couple of snotty remarks by people who [didn't] know what they are talking about and [spoke] as if the bog images were picked up for convenience instead of being . . . a deeply felt part of my own life, a revelation to me."[6] "Relic of Memory," for example, appeared in *Door into the Dark,* and although the geography of the poem concerns loughs

77

rather than bogs, Heaney is clearly intent on representing the preserving powers of his landscape:

> The lough waters
> Can petrify wood:
> Old oars and posts
> Over the years
> Harden their grain,
> Incarcerate ghosts
>
> Of sap and season.
> The shallows lap
> And give and take—
> Constant ablutions,
> Such drowning love
> Stun a stake
>
> To stalagmite. . . .

The loughs, the geographical analogy of the memory, accept, modify, and return a culture's offerings, its "oars and posts." The poem ends by describing the "relic" from the bog that first held his attention: "A piece of stone/On the shelf at school,/Oatmeal coloured." Fifteen years later, in "Sandstone Keepsake," a poem included in *Station Island,* Heaney describes a piece of sandstone that he has found while wading the beach at Inishowen, and the poem, depicting the poet as both the preserver of culture and the lonely wanderer, provides an example of how the imaginative life demands solitude, a life that—to use Auden's phrase—makes nothing happen. Even though the poem ultimately contemplates the poet as a solitary wanderer and not as in "Relic of Memory," the stone itself, the poet still appears as a harmless collector, one "not about to set times wrong or right,/Stooping along, one of the venerators." However complex the political implications of Heaney's verse become, a consoling number of poems depict the poet alone in his environment, quietly drawing strength from the solitude of the countryside, a solitude that cultivates, as Heaney puts it, the art of veneration. Lonely poets who wander through the countryside or wade along the shoreline pressing poems from their vigils find their analogue in the shepherds of pastoral literature who followed their flocks through the fields and played their pipes as they went. Solitude, along with nostalgia and love, represents another characteristic of the pastoral that finds a prominent place in Heaney's work.

Whether dispossessed of farmland in Italy, or battening flocks at Horton, or wandering in the Cumner hills, the farmers, shepherds, and gypsies of English literature often reside in their cottages, pastures, and camps with a polemical resignation. And if they have not been driven to their solitude, their solitude often seems fragile, anxiously aware of the corrupting world that may intrude at any time. Even Wordsworth's Michael, a pastoralist of the first order, is bound in surety to his brother's son, an agreement that drastically alters the covenant with nature that the old shepherd has tended for so long. Narcissism, a danger that received the most cursory investigation by Clare and Heaney, faces the unwary loner, and pastoral literature is rich with examples of vainglorious intro-spection—it is an occupational hazard for the wandering shepherd. But solitude also leads to self-knowledge, as it did in "Sandstone Keep-sake," and for Heaney this ultimately results in a broader, more assimila-tive vision of his race.

In "Shoreline," another poem from *Door into the Dark,* Heaney refines his stance as a solitary wanderer. The poem begins with a charac-teristic piece of landscape description—colloquial, rhythmic, and un-peopled:

> Turning a corner, taking a hill
> In County Down, there's the sea
> Sidling and settling to
> The back of a hedge. Or else
>
> A grey bottom with puddles
> Dead-eyed as fish.
> Haphazard tidal craters march
> The corn and the grazing.

And the poet, after two stanzas of sketching the expansive coastline, sharpens his focus again, developing the genealogical concern, here in its infancy, that will come to dominate *North:*

> Take any minute. A tide
> Is rummaging in
> At the foot of all fields,
> All cliffs and shingles.

Listen. Is it the Danes,
A black hawk bent on the sail?
Or the chinking Normans?
Or currachs hopping high

On to the sand?
Strangford, Arklow, Carrickfergus,
Belmullet and Ventry
Stay, forgotten like sentries.

"Is it the Danes. . . ?" In a more sober moment, the question seems forced and sentimentally rhetorical. And even when taken seriously, it begs rather than elicits a sympathetic complicity from the reader. No Vikings are on the beach. But the question is a pivotal one in Heaney's work because it represents his first attempt to move from landscape to genealogy, from the present moment to a past age. Solitude here is giving way to a larger sense of an ancestral community. The present moment, impregnated with associations deriving from a harsh, northern culture, avoids the descriptive embellishment that often accompanies nostalgic sentimentality. Heaney's version of pastoral nostalgia is an ironic one because his backward glance, so assuaging to the traditional pastoralist, discovers a bellicose society, but one that nonetheless offers Heaney a convincing cultural analogue.

Door into the Dark closes with two poems that prefigure the poetic strategies that will culminate in *North,* strategies that memorialize the various elements of landscape in ways that recall familiar pastoral situations. In "Bann Clay," for example, Heaney speaks ominously of "it":

Labourers pedalling at ease
Past the end of the lane
Were white with it. Dungarees
And boots wore its powdery stain . . .

It underruns the valley,
The first slow residue
Of a river finding its way.
Above it, the webbed marsh is new,

Even the clutch of Mesolithic
Flints. . . .

Even the "Mesolithic flints," those prehistoric relics, lie over and above the clay that "underruns the valley." As the symbol of a people indentured to their land, the Bann clay, saturating the clothes of the farmers, recalls its more prominent ancestor in County Monaghan where Patrick Kavanagh had begun *The Great Hunger* with the simple assertion, "Clay is the word and clay is the flesh. . . ." Kavanagh's work occasionally provides the model for understanding Heaney's poetic methods, and one example in particular succinctly illustrates how a distinctive feature of the Irish landscape becomes synonymous with the culture itself. In Kavanagh's novel, *Tarry Flynn,* a record of one poet's adolescence in rural Ireland and a fitting introduction to the polemical provincialism that underlies much of Heaney's writing, Kavanagh repeats the syntactic patterns of his poem's opening gambit and applies it to a description of a church's congregation: "It was a squalid grey-faced throng. The sunlight through the coloured windows played on that congregation but could not smooth parchment faces and wrinkled necks to polished ivory. *Skin was the color of clay, and clay was in their hair and clothes.* The little tillage fields went to Mass" (emphasis added).[7] The Ireland of *Tarry Flynn* is filled with the dreaming days of a young boy, and the clay alone is enough to recall the transcendent joys of a rural childhood; but pastoral literature always subverts its gleaming vision, and, as Kavanagh knows, the clay of Monaghan returns to dust.

Throughout Kavanagh's writing, the large issues of religion and identity emanate from the squalid detail of his descriptions. But transcendence, religious or secular, is rare both in the poetry and the prose because the poetry and the prose are bent to the same task—elucidating the aspects of life in rural Ireland that make transcendence difficult. As a result, the work exudes a sobering iconoclasm, exposing the thoroughgoing English-bred lie known as the Irish Literary Revival. But great care is taken by both Kavanagh and Heaney to prepare their childhood landscapes, to ready them for the important role they will assume in their later work.

"Bogland," the poem that closes *Door into the Dark,* offers the first extended description of a bog, the topography that will dominate much of the poetry. As in "Bann Clay," or as in *Tarry Flynn,* the poem's organizing metaphor resists heavenly ascensions—what rises in this poem rises from a "bottomless" pit to the lowest surfaces of the earth. Yet the bogs provide Heaney with the link to the Iron Age culture situated at the base of his imaginative genealogy. Like Kavanagh's clay, Heaney's bog is the great negator, continually qualifying specious magnanimities by reminding us of our earthly origins. The poem begins in negation:

> We have no prairies
> To slice a big sun at evening—
> Everywhere the eye concedes to
> Encroaching horizon,
>
> Is wooed into the cyclops' eye
> Of a tarn. Our unfenced country
> Is bog that keeps crusting
> Between the sights of the sun.

The admission that opens the poem—"We have no prairies"—implicitly compares two landscapes, one pocked with bogs, the other flattened by prairies. A note of benevolent separatism sharpens the comparison as Heaney alludes both to the American pioneers and to the Irish farmers digging peat in the bogs; the first word of the following passage receives a full stress to heighten the comparison:

> Our pioneers keep striking
> Inwards and downwards,
>
> Every layer they strip
> Seems camped on before.
> The bogholes might be Atlantic seepage.
> The wet centre is bottomless.

The poem is important because it represents Heaney's earliest musings on a topographical metaphor that will assume extraordinary significance in Heaney's attempt to locate a precedent for the violent struggles that have plagued Northern Ireland since the partition agreement of 1921. The deep, densely layered "bogholes" differ sharply from the wide, flat prairies; by juxtaposing the two geographies, Heaney distinguishes the bogs of Ireland from another prominent landscape that weighs heavily on another national imagination. Much of the poem's significance lies in the act of reclaiming the bogs both as a subject for poetry and as a central metaphor that will organize that poetry. Reclamation, then, becomes the burden of Heaney's imagination as it furnishes the poet with an imaginative representation of a past era, an era whose ancient ways might form the basis for a dramatic and cogent response to the divisive problems of his own country. As he reclaims his racial origins through his poems, he attempts to restore a measure of historical understanding to the problem; and the hope of restoration, as Virgil demonstrated in "Eclogue I," is the hope of pastoral nostalgia.

The four poems just examined ("Relic of Memory," "Shoreline," "Bann Clay," and "Bogland") cultivated seminal versions of themes and images that will persist, gaining both in their powers of implication and reference, throughout *North*. These poems were predominantly historical in their orientation; yet "Ocean's Love to Ireland" combined history, language, and eroticism to depict a world of pastoral perfection as it stood poised at the moment of pillage. Several of the poems that begin *Wintering Out* further develop two of these concerns—history and language—and establish a mythology based on etymology, the science devoted to reconstructing the historical development of a word. In "Anahorish," a poem already examined for its use of place names, a simple verbal sound suggests to the poet images of historical significance:

> My 'place of clear water,'
> the first hill in the world
> where springs washed into
> the shiny grass
>
> and darkened cobbles
> in the bed of the lane.
> *Anahorish*, soft gradient
> of consonant, vowel-meadow,
>
> after-image of lamps
> swung through the yards
> on winter evenings.
> With pails and barrows
>
> those mound-dwellers
> go waist-deep in mist
> to break the light ice
> at wells and dunghills.

The opening lines recall the familiar wells of "Personal Helicon," and the pristine quality of "the first hill in the world" suggests the Arcadian context of pastoral. The succession of images that follows Heaney's pronunciation of the word "Anahorish" seems largely associational in its logic, but these associations lead from the secluded, intensely personal memory of a young boy at a well to the larger racial memory that insists on the presence of ancestors, "those mound dwellers." And midway between the young boy and his ancestors stands "*Anahorish,* soft gradient/Of consonant, vowel-meadow. . . ." Heaney mediates personal experience with a national past by using the mellifluous sounds of a place name to begin such a meditation. History for Heaney becomes a subtle meshing of language and lineage.

Anecdotal histories are countered by themes drawn from accredited histories, a technique that allows the pastoral to develop a sustaining myth while insinuating and glancing—to use Puttenham's original formulation—at other matters. "The Wool Trade" begins with an epigraph excerpted from the fifth section of *A Portrait of the Artist as a Young Man:* "How different are the words 'home,' 'Christ,' 'ale,' 'master,' on his lips and mine." But the passage in the novel that precedes this one is the better known of the two. The dean of the school is speaking to Stephen:

> To return to the lamp, he said, the feeding of it is also a nice problem. You must choose the pure oil and you must be careful when you pour it in not to overflow it, not to pour in more than the funnel can hold.
> What funnel? asked Stephen.
> The funnel through which you pour the oil into your lamp.
> That? said Stephen. Is that called a funnel? Is it not a tundish?
> What is a tundish?
> That. The . . . funnel.
> Is that called a tundish in Ireland? asked the dean. I never heard the word in my life.
> It is called a tundish in lower Drumcondra, said Stephen laughing, where they speak the best English.
> A tundish, said the dean reflectively. That is a most interesting word. I must look that word up. Upon my word I must.[8]

The word "interesting" condescends as the phrase "upon my word" patronizes. Following the passage that Heaney chose for his epigraph, Dedalus remarks bitterly, "His [the dean's] language, so familiar and so foreign, will always be for me an acquired speech. . . . My soul frets in the shadow of his language." Clearly, perhaps obviously, the political ramifications of England's linguistic imperialism dominate both the passage from the novel and the poem, which ends:

O all the hamlets where
Hills and flocks and streams conspired

To a language of waterwheels,
A lost syntax of looms and spindles,

How they hang
Fading, in the gallery of the tongue!

And I must talk of tweed,
A stiff cloth with flecks like blood.

Successful military invasions often result in the enforcement or gradual encroachment—both conditions exist—of the victor's language, and Joyce and Heaney are drawn to those incidents in the daily life of an Irishman where language and political history overlap. But Heaney's Ireland is kinder than Joyce's. It is a region whose invigorating geographies kindle the hope of resistance, of conspiracy; it is a place where "Hills and flocks and streams conspired/To a language of waterwheels,/ A lost syntax of looms and spindles. . . ." Heaney imagines here an idealized language, a kind of "shape-note language," as he describes a similar notion in "Alphabets," a poem from *The Haw Lantern* (1987). Here, in "The Wool Trade," the world of concrete objects, the fodder for metaphor, "conspires" in the poet's dream to become an unspoiled field of reference, presenting its own organized syntax of landscape and geography. Obviously the "hills and flocks," the diction of the poem, provide the traditional pastoral imagery, and, less obviously, the memory of these past times finds the poet looking over his shoulder, another pose essentially pastoral in its nostalgic perspective.

These historical and linguistic concerns do not always join seamlessly. "Traditions" began by confessing that Ireland's "guttural muse" was conquered long ago by the alliterative tradition in English literature, a linguistic assimilation analogous to the larger cultural assimilations forced by the conqueror's hand. This guttural sound though, like the Irish maid, has not been "bulled" into submission. The fourth section of "Gifts of Rain," concerning the Moyola River, precedes "Traditions" in *Wintering Out,* and by emphasizing the endurance of Ireland's trove of poetic metaphor, it softens the consonants landed by the alliterative assault. The speaker is "Dives," the name given to the man in the New Testament parable (Luke 16:19–31) who would not share his wealth with a poor man and who upon dying was sent to Hell:

> The tawny guttural water
> spells itself: Moyola
> is its own score and consort,
>
> bedding the locale
> in the utterance,
> reed music, an old chanter
>
> breathing its mists
> through vowels and history.
> A swollen river,
>
> a mating call of sound
> rises to pleasure me, Dives,
> hoarder of common ground.

"Dives," a Latin word, is associated with the parable but retains its sense of opulence and pagan celebration. The sound of the river "spells it-self . . . /bedding the locale/in the utterance." Heaney's depiction of the language and the locale, and particularly of their harmonious conjunction, provides the theoretical underpinnings for an English that would have pleased Stephen Dedalus as much as it would have "interested" his dean.

The Moyola River swells in Heaney's memory to mythic propor-tions, embodying the kind of earthly perfection found in pastoral land-scapes, but the river, "its own score and consort," offers Heaney a model for linguistic integrity as it rolls along unaffected by cultural upheaval, "an old chanter/breathing its mists/through vowels and history." Much of Heaney's verse, in fact, attempts to comprehend the landscape in terms of the verbal associations that the poet finds lurking there. The language found would be an enduring one, capable of extraordinary expression. Puttenham and the earliest pastoral theoreticians in England had exhaustively debated the question of pastoral language, and although their concern had been largely one of generic propriety, the pastoral world offered such seductive rewards to its citizens that its language must be equally powerful and persuasive. The dream of a perfected language belongs to the pastoral tradition.

The subject of language so dominates the poetry from the early to the mid-70s, that "tongues," difficult organs to describe, become important concrete details in several poems and allow Heaney to discover a natural transition between language and eroticism, two concerns that have traditionally distinguished pastoral literature. In "Toome," from *Wintering Out*, the tongue is set in motion by the pronunciation of the word, and the poem ends with an image that recalls Clare's passage on eels as well as the closing section of Heaney's "A Lough Neagh Sequence":

> My mouth holds round
> the soft blastings,
> *Toome, Toome,*
> as under the dislodged
>
> slab of the tongue
> I push into a souterrain
> prospecting what new
> in a hundred centuries'
>
> loams, flints, musket-balls,
> fragmented ware,
> torcs and fish-bones
> till I am sleeved in
>
> alluvial mud that shelves
> suddenly under
> bogwater and tributaries,
> and elvers tail my hair.

Subtly erotic connotations attend the "dislodged . . . tongue," as perhaps they do the body of a man being slowly "sleeved in/alluvial mud." The imagery of the poem ("loams, flints, musket-balls/fragmented ware,/torcs and fish-bones") recalls a distant and violent past, descending from modern musketry to ancient torcs. The pronunciation of the word "Toome" begins the meditation, and the sound of the word serves as a magical incantation, conjuring another world where eroticism, language, and landscape are so harmoniously enmeshed that the poet, "sleeved in alluvial mud," escapes to the environment that he imagines.

But pastoral enticements encourage defection, and the defector, traveling in strange lands, confronts the problem of every wandering monoglot. In imaginative terms, this blissful penetration of history's layers can often lead the same tongue to be "leashed in my throat," as Heaney phrases it in "Midnight." The poem concerns the disappearance of the wolf from Ireland, and its matter-of-fact style of reportage reveals a sympathy flexible enough to mourn the death of the wolf and romantic enough to eulogize Wolf Tone, the eighteenth-century Irish rebel:

> Since the professional wars—
> Corpse and carrion
> Paling in rain—
> The wolf has died out
>
> In Ireland. The packs
> Scoured parkland and moor
> Till a Quaker buck and his dogs
> Killed the last one
>
> In some scraggy waste of Kildare.
> The wolfhound was crossed
> With inferior strains,
> Forests coopered to wine casks.

Imagining the wolf's lair, Heaney continues:

> The old dens are soaking.
> The pads are lost or
> Retrieved by small vermin
>
> That glisten and scut.
> Nothing is panting, lolling,
> Vapouring. The tongue's
> leashed in my throat.

Allegorical republican sentiments need not dominate this poem. First, the poem is about wolves, and, second, about someone who, having identified himself with this Hughesian version of the imagination, feels frustrated by its eventual extinction. Such a poem, again focusing on the "tongue," revises the profuse satisfactions of "Toome" by depicting a

landscape at once harsher and less forgiving than the "alluvial mud" of
the earlier poem. Pastoral writing traditionally subverts its trumpeted
intentions, and taken together, these two poems provide a good example
of that particular tension.

Part one of *Wintering Out* contains the poems of high visibility,
the poems that have come to be associated with Heaney's early contri-
bution to English letters—"Fodder," "Anahorish," "Gifts of Rain,"
"Toome," "Traditions," "The Wool Trade," "A Northern Hoard,"
"Midnight," and "The Tollund Man," are all included here, and of
these, the last has created and occupied its own dominion in modern
letters. The poem responds powerfully to the photographs in Glob's *The
Bog People,* and they alone occasion wonder and curiosity. "The Tollund
Man" will figure prominently in the development of Heaney's Iron Age
mythology. The first section of the poem, however, develops the digni-
fied, muted eroticism of "Toome" and does so within a pastoral context.
The poem, while elaborating on the erotic theme hinted at earlier,
introduces the dominant concerns of Part two, the section often ignored
in discussions of the work. Five quatrains constitute the first of the
poem's three parts:

Some day I will go to Aarhus
To see his peat-brown head,
The mild pod of his eye-lids,
His pointed skin cap.

In the flat country nearby
Where they dug him out,
His last gruel of winter seeds
Caked in his stomach,

Naked except for
The cap, noose and girdle,
I will stand a long time.
Bridegroom to the goddess,

She tightened her torc on him
And opened her fen,
Those dark juices working
Him to a saint's kept body,

Trove of the turfcutters'
Honeycombed workings.
Now his stained face
Reposes at Aarhus.

The language describing the man portrays him as if he were a display case of the local flora—"peat-brown," "pods of his eye-lids," "winter seeds," and "honeycombed." The man's "rurality"—to use Clare's word—is the man's defining context, and part of the tension of this poem derives from Heaney's careful juxtaposition of the man's saintly innocence and his society's ritual violence. For Northern Ireland the phrase "innocent victim" has a terrible relevance, and Heaney's depiction of the Tollund Man exercises the peculiar sensibilities of a poet attempting to reconcile Republican dreams with the realities of occupation. When pastoral harmonies are disrupted, innocence is the glamorous victim. But innocence survives in the pastoral imagination, confronting the hostile world that would spoil it. This confrontation, continually pitting the simplicities of innocence against the moribund complexity of evil, assumes several guises in Heaney's poetry, but they rarely stray from this essential structure.

Simplicity, most always, is a willed illusion, and that is why pastoral writing often seems fantastic. Arcadian sex, for example, fascinates because the Golden Age might promise its citizens the boundless fulfillment of carnal desire. But Arcadianism is an inexact science, and the Golden Age might demand as well an unselfish devotion to honor and chastity. Both traditions are represented in the literature. Of all pastoral simplicities, sex seems the least simple and the most desirable. In "The Tollund Man," Heaney brings these issues in and out of focus, creating a network of associations that elucidate this particular aspect of pastoral writing. A "bridegroom to the goddess," the Tollund man has been offered as a sacrifice to her, and when she "open[s] her fen,/Those dark juices working/Him to a saint's kept body," the poem suggests the erotic aspects of sacrifice, of giving one's self wholly to another. Plunged into such extreme carnality, the man arises "a saint," as if purged of his mortal foibles by the violent ritual. The notion of purgation, of undergoing an experience, particularly a violent one, to understand, even to rid oneself of that experience, will recur in Heaney's writing as it does in much of the imaginative literature dealing with contemporary Northern Ireland. Purgation is the ennobling hope of the warrior, but its strategies for comprehending the enormity of ritual murder inform Heaney's portrait of the man from Tollund.

In Part two of *Wintering Out,* other poems present other erotic situations, all of them involving females who in various ways are associated with pastoral imagery. Three poems in particular depict the female exercising the idealized powers of a mythical figure and the practical sympathies of a mortal woman, a combination that works well in the tradition because of its willingness to contemplate simultaneously an envisioned paradise and the imperfect world that lies beyond its gilded gates. In "Summer Home," the poet and his family have taken up residence in a house, undergone an unnamed crisis, and by the poem's end, begun to emerge from it, healed. Of the five brief sections that constitute the poem, the third finds the couple in bed. In the previous section, the poet had arrived, "Bushing the door, [his] arms full/of wild cherry and rhododendron," but the floral bouquet cannot allay the "wound" sustained in the third section; nor can it stop the "thick healings" of sexual communion:

> O we tented our wound all right
> under the homely sheet
>
> and lay as if the cold flat of a blade
> had winded us.
>
> More and more I postulate
> thick healings, like now
>
> as you bend in the shower
> water lives down the tilting stoups of your breasts.

In the third section of "Summer Home," the hint of physical love— "postulate" suggests "copulate"—assumes reconciliatory, even ecclesiastical connotations—"stoups" stand in churches too. Love among the cherries and rhododendrons is not, for Heaney, Arcadian in its simplicity, but its physical mysteries alone bring a measure of graceful understanding, and it represents an enduring component of his pastoral.

Pastoral figures though are often tormented by the ordeal of their love. Milton set Orpheus's head floating "down the swift Hebrus," and the pathos of the Thracian's dismemberment at the hands of his ecstatic followers derives partly from the fact that Orpheus too had lost at love. In "A Winter's Tale," the second of the three poems depicting female figures in pastoral contexts, Heaney tells the story of a "lovely daughter" who ran "bare-breasted" from the door of the cottage. The neighbors found her huddled in bovine simplicity, and her "nakedness" seems to compliment her surroundings, as if an Arcadian grotesque is being described:

> Weeping, blood bright from her cuts
> Where she'd fled the hedged and wired
> Road, they eyed her nakedness
> Astray among the cattle
> At first light.

"Anahorish" described the "first hill in the world," and the "Winter's Tale" begins in "first light"—primacy, with its connotations of pristine beauty and unspoiled charm, complements the pastoral's vision of a Golden Age. Later in the poem, having described how the girl would flee from her home and enter the houses of her neighbors while they were away, Heaney tells us that when the neighbors returned to find her there, "Greetings passed/Between them. She was there first. . . ," another suggestion of her primacy. She had been sleeping "in the chimney nook," and when the owners of the house woke her, "She stirred as from a winter/Sleep. Smiled. Uncradled her breasts." A match for Persephone rising from the underworld in the spring, she appears here as a pastoral spirit, one whose sensual gesture might lead to the changing of the seasons.

Finally, in the third example an unnamed woman becomes involved in other, extreme situations, this time occurring both on or by the sea. "Shore Woman" is a monologue by a woman who recounts a fishing expedition with her husband. The couple has encountered a school of mackerel, and they "took them in at every cast," until suddenly, "the lines rose/Like a let-down," and the school was gone. Porpoises then surrounded them, and the woman, fearing that they would attack the boat, asks her husband to return to the shore. He refuses, and her story is a frightening one:

> . . . I lay and screamed
> Under splashed brine in an open rocking boat
> Feeling each dunt and slither through the timber,
> Sick at their huge pleasures in the water.

The final verse paragraph of the poem portrays the woman alone on the shore. From beginning to end, it maps her position as a wife, daughter, and woman of the community:

> I sometimes walk this strand for thanksgiving
> Or maybe it's to get away from him
> Skittering his spit across the stove. Here
> Is the taste of safety, the shelving sand
> Harbours no worse than razor-shell or crab—
> Though my father recalls carcasses of whales
> Collapsed and gasping, right up to the dunes.
> But to-night such moving sinewed dreams lie out
> In darker fathoms, far beyond the head.
> Astray upon a debris of scrubbed shells
> Between parched dunes and salivating wave,
> I have rights on this fallow avenue,
> A membrane between moonlight and my shadow.

Quickly, the poem moves from contemplating her earlier experiences to understanding her "rights on this fallow avenue. . . ." As a *genius loci,* she and her attributes are pared to a minimum; she resides among the "scrubbed shells" that lie between "parched dunes and salivating wave. . . ." As a dramatic character, she belongs in spirit to the long line of patient women whose patience derives not from living with a callous husband, and not from performing Herculean tasks around the house, but from her sympathetic—and to men, fearful—understanding of the complexities of natural cycles.

But such vestigial traces of the tradition are not the only evidences of pastoral found in *Wintering Out.* The second part of the collection contains several pieces more traditionally oriented in their overall sentiment and perspective than the poems just mentioned. These more obviously pastoral pieces are foreshadowed by "Navvy," a poem included near the end of the first section. A navvy, or a laborer, stands by the roadside, and begs a ride with the poet. Four years ago the "morass" to either side of the road "swallowed his yellow bulldozer/ . . . laying it down/with lake-dwellings and dug-outs,/pike-shafts, axe-heads, bone pins,/all he is indifferent to." Heaney's laborer, indifferent to archaeology and the sense of cultural tradition implied by that science, becomes a working-class hero, a character who typically exhibits the kind of skepticism concerning the literary endeavor that originally took Heaney from the farm:

> He has not relented
> under weather or insults,
> my brother and keeper

plugged to the hard-core,
picking along
the welted, stretchmarked
curve of the world.

The poem neatly exposes the problem inherent in most antipastoral writing since the nineteenth century. Poetry that claims an emotional sympathy with the worker or farmer traditionally runs the risk of claiming membership in their fraternity, a claim that the literary activity itself denies. Heaney's confessed skepticism concerning his literary art derives from this occupational conflict, and in a poem such as "Navvy," the conflict, if it surfaces at all, does so in ways too subtle to alter the sentimental note that mars the poem.

The poems in which Heaney openly admits to his long absence from the farm are at once the most nostalgic in their orientation and the least affected in their language. In "First Calf," for example, Heaney begins wistfully, "It's a long time since I saw," and continues in the next line, graphically, "afterbirth strung on the hedge. . . ." In the four quatrains of this poem, Heaney moves back and forth from the loving tones of fond recollection to the arresting details of the actual event, a combination of pastoral celebration and Crabbean realism that distinguished Clare's verse. And in "May," the poem that follows "First Calf," Heaney is again making the imaginative leap that gracefully expands the implications of a walk in the country. In the first stanza, the poet stands on a bridge and looks down at the trout in the brook; when the second stanza begins, he is in the water:

Wading green stems, lugs of leaf
That untangle and bruise
(Their tiny gushers of juice)
My toecaps sparkle now

Over the soft fontanel
Of Ireland. I should wear
Hide shoes, the hair next my skin,
For walking this ground. . . .

The vigorous creativity involved in comparing a stream in Ireland to the soft crease in a baby's skull insists, if not on an innocent Ireland, then at least on a pristine quality that hallows "this ground." Walking further, Heaney wonders, "Wasn't there a spa-well,/Its coping grassy, pendent?" And finally, the last quatrain, with its pastoral catalog of flowers, casts Heaney as a pilgrim, one longing to reinhabit the village that once stood here, an emblem of a lost, pastoral society:

> I'm out to find that village,
> Its low sills fragrant
> With ladysmock and celandine,
> Marshlights in the summer dark.

The conventions here are pastoral, the diction almost predictable. But the community sought here is Irish, and arriving near the end of *Wintering Out,* a book that has essentially redefined pastoral nostalgia, the poem bristles with an exuberant confidence.

The rural community depicted in "A Winter's Tale" lay far from the traditional pastoral community, and Heaney seems always ready to engage his talents in the depiction of the alienated soul, the deprived child of nature. In a poem like "Bye Child," the pastoral lineage seems to have dwindled to the point of insignificance, but an analysis of the poem's diction reveals an impressive level of implication surrounding this dire rural vignette. The diction exhibits Heaney's ability to organize the various elements of the vignette to form a pointed comment on subjects that would seem otherwise beyond its purview. This, as Virgil first demonstrated, and as Puttenham first recognized, is the essence of pastoral writing. In "Bye Child," Heaney relates the story of a young man who has been raised in a henhouse. The epigraph to the poem is succinct: "He was discovered in the henhouse where she had confined him. He was incapable of saying anything." The last two stanzas of the poem follow a description of the boy's living quarters. His mother, who is walking away from the henhouse, has just fed him:

> After those footsteps, silence;
> Vigils, solitudes, fasts,
> Unchristened tears,
> A puzzled love of the light.
> But now you speak at last
>
> With a remote mime
> Of something beyond patience,
> Your gaping wordless proof
> Of lunar distances
> Travelled beyond love.

Heaney imagines a boy accustomed to vigils, solitudes, and fasts, words whose connotations, when removed from the context of a henhouse, have a sobering significance for the citizens of Northern Ireland. In the *New Statesman* article mentioned previously, Heaney had written about the odd, gangrenous "doublethink" that operates in Belfast, where many feel that "something is rotten, but maybe if we wait it will fester to death."[9] Such a destructive patience may well serve as the thin disguise of a frightened apathy, but when the boy's face reveals to Heaney "something beyond patience," the political context begins to assert its defining presence through the situation chosen to depict the boy in the henhouse. The pastoral imagination, when it works most effectively, seems innately, even naively, drawn to those rural vignettes richly endowed with implication. The odd, orphaned boy, severed from all form of spoken or written language, seems a distant but kindred spirit to the Irish poet, removed from his own language and forced to speak English, his "acquired" speech, as Dedalus has it. Silence, "something beyond patience," and exile—these are the watchwords of political resistance, and, here, urging endurance, they belong to the sobering world of the antipastoral, a nightmarish vision of a voiceless culture.

Such a poem approaches the condition of allegory, and the subject of political allegory is a common one whenever Heaney's work is discussed. It has most often affected evaluations of the two poems that open and close the first section of *North*. Both "Antaeus" and "Hercules and Antaeus," one a monologue by Antaeus, the other a third-person narrative, encourage the traditional, allegorical interpretation. Antaeus, the giant who lived in Libya, guarded a pass and had to be wrestled by travelers wishing to proceed with their journey. The travelers, however, were unaware of the fact that the giant gained strength every time he was thrown and touched the earth, his mother. Hercules's victory over Antaeus was initially an intellectual one because he discovered that holding the giant over his head would cause his eventual downfall. The first three stanzas of the poem introduce the giant, emphasizing the strengths he derives from his terrestrial allegiances:

> When I lie on the ground
> I rise flushed as a rose in the morning.
> In fights I arrange a fall on the ring
> To rub myself with sand
>
> That is operative
> As an elixir. I cannot be weaned

> Off the earth's long contour, her river-veins.
> Down here in my cave
>
> Girdered with root and rock
> I am cradled in the dark that wombed me
> And nurtured in every artery
> Like a small hillock.

"I cannot be weaned/Off the earth's long contour"—the phrase recalls a similar umbilical attachment in "Navvy," where the laborer was "picking along/the welted, stretchmarked/curve of the world." Earth-dwellers, whether mythological or actual, are reserved a sympathetic place in Heaney's poetry, and Antaeus seems an overly endowed navvy. Nurtured "like a small hillock"—a peculiarly old-fashioned coinage, redolent of musty pastoral—Antaeus becomes in Heaney's description someone enthralled by the earth, and although to claim the poem solely for pastoral might even contort this tradition's readily flexible boundaries, the devotions to the land itself, when it becomes a political issue, is not far removed from one of the genre's central obsessions.

Both Heaney and his commentators have spoken eloquently about the neat parallels between Antaeus, the brooding, strength overthrown by the "sky-born and royal" Hercules, and the brooding Ireland overthrown time and again by England. These are poems about "colonization," suggests Blake Morrison, and they could be read "as an allegory of the Protestant settlement of Ireland":[10]

> Sky-born and royal,
> snake-choker, dung-heaver,
> his mind big with golden apples,
> his future hung with trophies,
>
> Hercules has the measure
> of resistance and black powers
> feeding off the territory.
> Antaeus, the mould-hugger,
>
> is weaned at last:
> a fall was a renewal
> but now he is raised up—
> the challenger's intelligence
>
> is a spur of light. . . .

So begins "Hercules and Antaeus," the poem that closes the first section of *North*. The emphasis on the powers and the mysteries of the earth makes a fitting introduction and conclusion to the bog poems—both the Tollund Man and Antaeus are connected with the powers of earth, the one preservative, the other resuscitative, and both lie vanquished by an act of violence. However persuasive these national allegories may seem, these stanzas are reductive nonetheless, simplifying the history—as allegory must—and rendering it formulaic and obtrusive. Several other stanzas of "Hercules and Antaeus" more clearly divulge the informing logic of this sequence, and, with their emphasis on loss and origin, they provide a moving portrayal of the emotional origins of pastoral:

> the challenger's intelligence
>
> is a spur of light,
> a blue prong graiping him
> out of his element
> into a dream of loss
>
> and origins—the cradling dark,
> the river-veins, the secret gullies
> of his strength,
> the hatching grounds
>
> of cave and souterrain,
> he has bequeathed it all
> to elegists. . . .

The elegy, originally a pastoral form, gains strength when Antaeus is forced to conjure "a dream of loss/and origins," the quintessential pastoral dream that arises when Golden Ages are envisioned. The poems that describe this version of nostalgia, that supply the historical details of the myth that Heaney constructs, are the poems devoted to the bog people.

"The Tollund Man," from *Wintering Out*, "Bog Queen," and "The Grauballe Man," both from *North*, combine to form a triumvirate from the Danish bogs. Read as a group, the poems demonstrate how Heaney's conception of the Iron Age evolves into the flexible myth that orders his understanding of contemporary Ireland. What is its ultimate significance in the overall scheme of ideas presented by the poetry? And how do they develop the pastoral? The characterization of "The Tollund Man" was ultimately tied to pastoral images, both floral and sexual. As in "May," where Heaney appeared as a pilgrim of sorts, searching for a lost village, Heaney begins "The Tollund Man" with the simple declaration, "Someday I will go to Aarhus," a similarly peripatetic posture. The second section of the poem, which chronicles the legend concerning the fate of four Republicans killed during the 1920s in Northern Ireland, begins with the note of hesitation that began the first section:

> I could risk blasphemy,
> Consecrate the cauldron bog
> Our holy ground and pray
> Him to make germinate
>
> The scattered, ambushed
> Flesh of labourers,
> Stockinged corpses
> Laid out in the farmyards,
>
> Tell-tale skin and teeth
> Flecking the sleepers
> Of four young brothers, trailed
> For miles along the lines.

In the third and final section, the poet hopes that "something of his sad freedom/As he rode the tumbril/Should come to me. . . ." Notes of hesitation and wishing, traces of the optative mood, have accumulated quickly—"Someday I will go," "I could risk blasphemy," "Should come to me"—and this mood persists even into *The Haw Lantern,* when he describes his community in "From the Canton of Expectation" as living "deep in a land of optative moods." When Heaney prays to the Tollund man to make the corpses of the young Republicans "germinate," he draws hopeful parallels, as has been often pointed out, between the ritual killing and fertility rites of the Iron Age and the ritual killing and sectarian violence of contemporary Northern Ireland. Heaney's interest in this ancient and barbarous culture was part of a growing interest in the political implications of Celtic archaism in general. In Jutland, a province of Denmark, Heaney will feel "lost,/Unhappy and at home" because he will have ironically fulfilled his nostalgic wishes. He will have returned to the original altars of violence still claiming their victims in Northern Ireland.

The optative mood necessarily circumscribes the Republican spirit that survives in Northern Ireland. The wishing verb carefully inserted at the beginning of each of the three sections of the poem retains the wistful distance of pastoral nostalgia that resists the confident note of the indicative mood. But pastoral, particularly pastoral nostalgia, begins with a sense of loss, and concurrently, a sense of longing to repair that loss. Throughout the literature, this desire to restore the past has been accompanied by the sobering realization that such a restoration is impossible, and these antithetical desires and realizations found their most dramatic presentation in pastoral writing. When Heaney imaginatively discovers the reconciliatory potential of the Tollund man, when he traces a genealogical ancestor that might explain the violence in Northern Ireland, and when he finds simultaneously that his ancestors' promises are being kept on the streets of Belfast, he has aligned himself with one of the subversive paradoxes that has defined much pastoral literature.

The second poem of the triumvirate, "Bog Queen," is a monologue, spoken by the Queen. Like the Tollund Man, she is a creature of the environment, her body recording the ebb and flow of the natural cycles:

> My body was braille
> for the creeping influences:
> dawn suns groped over my head
> and cooled at my feet,
>
> through my fabrics and skins
> the seeps of winter
> digested me,
> the illiterate roots
>
> pondered and died
> in the cavings
> of stomach and socket. . . .

The poem had begun on a more ominous note; the Queen "lay waiting/between turf-face and demesne wall," until a turfcutter's spade "barbered/and stripped" her and she "rose," as the poem closes, "from the dark,/hacked bone, skull-ware,/frayed stitches, tufts,/small gleams on the bank." Her grave plundered, the Queen ascends, but her ascension is not accompanied by the glorious fanfare normally accorded such transubstantial affairs. Her appearance in the bog is occasioned by economic need—the turfcutters find her as they gather fuel for the winter.

As in "Navvy," where the laborer picked along "the stretchmarked/ curve of the world," as in "Antaeus," where the giant could not be weaned from "the earth's long contour," so here, the Queen, for all her verve and vigor, assumes a geographical anonymity that lends her the impersonal power of a historical cycle, of an era.

These speaking spirits represent a kind of politically savvy pathetic fallacy and establish a clear link with one of Clare's most distinctive works, a poem that supplies an instructive parallel to several strategies deployed by Heaney in "Bog Queen." Although the voice of the poem is clearly meant to be the Queen's voice, her voice intones a grand environmental hymn, and when Heaney reviewed an anthology of pastoral poetry in 1975, he singled out Clare's "The Lament of Swordy Well" for extravagant praise, claiming that it "must be one of the best poems of its century."[11] Swordy Well, commonly known as Swaddy Well, was an ancient stone quarry used by the Romans, and it was best known for its wildflowers and butterflies. Enclosure befell Swordy Well, and to commemorate the loss Clare wrote a monologue spoken by this historical ground. "The Lament of Swordy Well," like "Bog Queen," is cast in quatrains, and the rhetoric of the poem is frequently the rhetoric of the politically oppressed:[12]

> Im swordy well a piece of land
> Thats fell upon the town
> Who worked me till I couldnt stand
> & crush me now Im down
>
> There was a time my bit of ground
> Made freeman of the slave
> The ass no pindard dare to pound
> When I his supper gave
>
> The gipseys camp was not affraid
> I made his dwelling free
> Till vile enclosure came and made
> A parish slave of me

A foreboding prophecy accompanies the closing, pristine vision of Swordy Well:

> To keep my hills from cart and plough
> & strife of mongerel men

& as spring found me find me now
I should look up agen

& save his Lordships woods that past
the day of danger dwell
Of all the fields I am the last
that my own face can tell

Yet what with stone pits delving holes
& strife to buy & sell
My name will quickly be the whole thing
Thats left of swordy well

The "cart and plough," the spring season that finds the old quarry unaltered through the ages, the "mongerel men" who will spoil the hillside, and the final warning that such cloistered beauty will soon disappear—these are the images and concerns of all pastoral writers who prefer the luxuriant, even virginal, landscape that has repaired to the imagination's visionary kingdom. Dispossession, whether of a dream or an acre, is countered with insurgency, imaginative or political. At times, the language of "Swordy Well" speaks as much for the small farmer as for the land itself:

Though Im no man yet any wrong
Some sort of right may seek
& I am glad if een a song
Gives me the room to speak

Both "The Bog Queen" and "The Lament of Swordy Well" preserve the spirit of a locality by giving it a voice. The ethics of articulation must concern any writer who would speak for the newly enfranchised society, and that is why pastoral writing, which must imagine an Edenic linguistics, was often accused of artificiality. Both Clare and Heaney become artful ventriloquists in these poems, and although their landscapes speak of different pasts, their stories depend strongly on the nostalgic hope that the old ways might serve as the tutelary spirit for their own societies.

"The Grauballe Man," the last of the three poems that deals specifically with the bog people, begins as the other two began by comparing the man's anatomy to various features or inhabitants of the landscape. His wrists are grained "like bog oak," his heel resembles a "basalt egg," and his arches have shrunk, "cold as a swan's foot/or a wet swamp root." The implicit hope of "The Tollund Man" was that the sectarian violence of Northern Ireland might be transformed into a fertility rite, promising peace and bounty for the future, as the sacrificial victim presaged for his age. In "The Grauballe Man," this hope has assumed the confident stance of a rhetorical question:

> Who will say 'corpse'
> To his vivid cast?
> Who will say 'body'
> to his opaque repose?

For Heaney, this "corpse," this "body," reposes at the bottom of his consoling mythology, providing him with a historical context for the political problems currently facing Northern Ireland. Invested with Heaney's mythopoeic energies, the man is no longer a "corpse." His "opaque repose" has suggested to the poet a revitalizing interpretation of Irish history because the man belongs now to the "memory," both in the personal and racial dimension:

> I first saw his twisted face
>
> in a photograph,
> a head and shoulder
> out of the peat,
> bruised like a forceps baby,
>
> but now he lies
> perfected in my memory,
> down to the red horn
> of his nails,
>
> hung in the scales
> with beauty and atrocity. . . .

In twentieth-century Ireland, the scales of beauty and atrocity are perilously balanced. The spring season, encompassing both the Ascension ritual of the Christian church and the Bacchic revelries of pagan society, celebrates the rejuvenation of the world. It is difficult to imagine the Grauballe man in his Easter finery. But the dolorous refrain of Yeats's "Easter, 1916," warning that "a terrible beauty is born," is echoed here by Heaney and suggests that Heaney's perfecting memory, as it fashions a grisly nostalgia piece, will bring the force of his cultural tradition, the "actual weight/of each hooded victim," to bear on his understanding of contemporary Northern Ireland. Edna Longley, in an otherwise helpful essay on *North,* remarks that "beauty on the whole has outweighed atrocity" in these lines;[13] such perhaps is the hope of the poem, but just as the birth imagery of "Easter, 1916" suggests a difficult and trying period of labor, so the Grauballe man is "bruised like a forceps baby." And this uncertainty concerning the efficacy of sacrifice, whether politically or ritually oriented, establishes the dominant tone of the poem.

Both Yeats and Heaney are concerned here with the fears and hopes attending cataclysmic change. The Republicans of the early twentieth century handed Yeats the grandiose assumptions of political revolution, while the Grauballe man effects quieter, less noisy changes in Heaney's ideas concerning an "adequate" poetry. Both events, however, were quickly submitted to the refining fires of the poetic imagination and emerged as enameled objects, clinging to their verisimilitude through the force of their creator's will. The Grauballe man, Heaney intones, "lies/ perfected in my memory," while Yeats's wisdom concerning the Republicans seems equally detached from its acknowledged subject when he confesses, as the poem closes, that it is "enough/To know they dreamed and are dead." Having discovered a rude beauty, and having seen that rude beauty lost, both poets resort to the nostalgic restoration of an heroic age. Whether in the city of Dublin or near the village of Grauballe, Yeats and Heaney nurture the saving resonances of legend, martyrdom, and an idealizing mythology. To the extent that they have relegated these legends, martyrdoms, and mythologies to the past, and to the extent that they have returned wistfully and hopefully in their poetry, they have given us another version of nostalgia.

The act of returning has provided the definitive moment for several of Heaney's poems. He assumed the pilgrim's posture, for example, in "The Tollund Man" and "May"; "North," the title poem of its volume, begins:

> I returned to a long strand,
> the hammered shod of a bay,
> and found only the secular
> powers of the Atlantic thundering.

Writers who record an imaginative return or escape to climates more accommodating than those presently inhabited are following the traditional trail of pastoral literature. Part of Heaney's revision of pastoral writing has been climatic in kind—the climates of the traditional Golden Age, although sympathetic, warm, and nurturing, have not fostered for him the resurgence of hope and well-being that his cold, northern climates have. As a result, Heaney's nostalgia, his conserving "hindsight," derives from Nordic traditions—sober, dire, and harsh, yet epiphanic in their effects:

> I faced the unmagical
> invitations of Iceland,
> the pathetic colonies
> of Greenland, and suddenly
>
> those fabulous raiders,
> those lying in Orkney and Dublin
> measured against
> their long swords rusting,
>
> those in the solid
> belly of stone ships,
> those hacked and glinting
> in the gravel and thawed streams
>
> were ocean-deafened voices
> warning me, lifted again
> in violence and epiphany.
> The longship's swimming tongue
>
> was buoyant with hindsight. . . .

The poem continues with phrases and images that, like the other poems, carry connotations enriched by the context of contemporary Irish history. When Thor's hammer "swung/to geography and trade," Ireland's long-standing economic connections with northern Europe and England receive their mythological sanction. And the tired desperation arising from an abandoned struggle permeates the poem when Heaney states flatly that "exhaustions nominated peace,/memory incubating the spilled blood." Much like the language of traditional pastoral, the diction that Heaney has crafted seems naturally bound to the subject of the Norse invasion but nonetheless retains the flexibility demanded by the art of implication, a pastoral *sine qua non*. This flexibility, which gives the verse the freedom to establish connections between Viking raiders and contemporary paramilitaries, is one of the important elements of any poetry that would further the development of the tradition.

"Belderg," one of the first poems of *North*, seems appropriately read as a coda to the bog poems, because it moves from a contemplation of the poet's racial past to an understanding of the narrower confines of his boyhood home. Although clearly related to the Iron Age bog culture, the subject of the poem derives from the discovery of "quernstones," stones with a hollowed depression in them that held the grains ground to flour and meal. The main action of the poem takes place in the house of a collector, one who has amassed an array of these stones, and the collector's voice begins the poem:

> 'They just kept turning up
> And were thought of as foreign'—
> One-eyed and benign
> They lie about his house,
> Quernstones out of a bog.
>
> To lift the lid of the peat
> And find this pupil dreaming
> Of neolithic wheat!
> When he stripped off blanket bog
> The soft-piled centuries
>
> Fell open like a glib:
> There were the first plough-marks,
> The stone-age fields, the tomb
> Corbelled, turfed and chambered,
> Floored with dry turf-coomb.

The "pupil," the quernstone, is "dreaming" about the grains it once held. In "The Grauballe Man," the body had been "perfected" in Heaney's memory, and in Yeats's "Easter, 1916," the poet had inherited the inspired "dreams" of the Irish rebels; here, the stone, Heaney's "pupil" to the past, resurrects the culture from which it came. As an artifact, the stone instigates the familiar process of excavation, of recovering the lost lineaments of his racial history; Heaney's version of pastoral nostalgia often ends in a linguistic variation of that theme:

Before I turned to go

He talked about persistence,
A congruence of lives,
How, stubbed and cleared of stones,
His home accrued growth rings
Of iron, flint and bronze.

So I talked of Mossbawn,
A bogland name. "But *moss?*"
He crossed my old home's music
With older strains of Norse.
I'd told how its foundation

Was mutable as sound
And how I could derive
A forked root from that ground
And make *bawn* an English fort,
A planter's walled-in mound,

Or else find sanctuary
And think of it as Irish,
Persistent if outworn.

From quernstones to the name of his family home, Heaney's past ripples with political insinuation. The "moss" and "bawn," forming the name of the poet's family farm, represent yet another version of Heaney's etymological nostalgia. This distinctive sensibility leads the poet to find even in the rural splendors of his childhood home an emblem of Northern Ireland's divided culture. In the third part of "Belfast," the second essay of *Preoccupations,* Heaney provides a fuller account of his home's etymology:

Our farm was called Mossbawn. *Moss,* a Scots word probably carried to Ulster by the Planters, and *bawn,* the name the English colonists gave to their fortified farmhouses. Mossbawn, the planter's house on the bog. Yet in spite of this Ordnance of Survey spelling, we pronounced it Moss bann, and *ban* is the Gaelic word for white. So might not the thing mean the white moss, the moss of bog-cotton? In the syllables of my home I see a metaphor of the split culture of Ulster.

107

Heaney's attempt to subvert the English pedigree of the word depends upon the Gaelic language, and that language, with the prominent role it had played in conceiving the need for a Republic, has become synonymous with Ireland's cultural renovation in the early twentieth century. Its presence on the school syllabus is in one sense a legitimate and national nostalgia. When the poem ends, Heaney again repairs to an imagined past, as he passes "through the eye of the quern," seeing in his "mind's eye . . . /A world-tree of balanced stones,/Querns piled like vertebrae,/The marrow crushed to grounds." Making stone implements, grinding grain, living around the bogs—the people and the culture that breed Heaney's "world-tree" are not the people of Virgil's Golden Age. They represent in many ways the emotional antithesis of the gleaming benevolence that Virgil had predicted for Augustus's reign. But Virgil, a poet of such consummate political sensibilities that he has been called a toady, was concerned to celebrate the glories of the Roman empire on his own terms, and like Heaney he fashioned an imaginative vision of his country's distant past that facilitated his qualified celebration. Heaney, who sees a dim present clouded by a dimmer future, resorts to myths and histories that would explain his predicament and so comfort the sufferer, and these myths and histories represent an ironic reversal of the traditional—Virgilian—pastoral perspective. But the imaginative direction, the strategies that govern the rural imagery, and the consolations derived from their nurturing nostalgias are remarkably similar to Virgil's pastoral both in technique and, most important of all, in their generic orientation.

Politic, Cautious, and Meticulous:
Pastoral Contexts in *Field Work* and *Station Island*

Because the term pastoral no longer refers to a restricted "kind" of literature—to use its original designation—it comprises a plethora of styles, themes, dictions, imageries, and literary forms that often seem unlikely heirs to the tradition. Even Puttenham showed a pedagogic zeal as he corrected his audience's misconceptions about the genre's authenticity—Theocritus's work is not, he argued, a dogged transcription of a goatherd's conversation, but a work of literary art, and a *highly* literary art at that. Various conventions of the genre have been extracted, recast, and reinvigorated in other, less obviously pastoral works, and Empson was the first critic in the twentieth century to sanction these remnants of the tradition by calling them "versions" of pastoral. For the past century, such inspired versions of pastoral represent our only pastorals, and in some of the poetry that Heaney wrote and collected from the mid-1970s to the mid-1980s, traces of the genre appear in isolated images and assumed contexts. Unlike much of the poetry of *North,* these traces reveal a conservative sensibility, one that seems intent on replacing the bold innovations of the earlier work with the older conventions habitually associated with the tradition. The second half of *North* provides isolated examples of these more conventional situations, and they provide the proper transition to the relevant poetry of *Field Work*, the subsequent volume. These glimpses of the older tradition, however, appear in radically revised contexts:

> Archimedes thought he could move the world if he could
> find the right place to position his lever. Billy Hunter
> said Tarzan shook the world when he jumped down out of a tree.

> I sink my crowbar in a chink I know under the masonry
> of state and statue, I swing on a creeper of secrets
> into the Bastille.

The opening lines of "The Unacknowledged Legislator's Dream," the poem which Heaney placed at the beginning of the second part of *North*, address the Romantic notion of the artist's unacknowledged, yet inspired, vision of political history. The poem's music depends on prose rhythms and the resolving final image depends on those familiar wild-eyed revolutionaries whose poetry occasions their captivity:

> In the cell, I wedge myself with outstretched arms
> in the corner and heave, I jump on the concrete flags to
> test them. Were those your eyes just now at the hatch?

In Ireland, these are the best of times to concoct this exotic specimen, the poet who wields a crowbar and attempts to assess the political situation of the country. From the Archimedean lever that begins the poem to the vaulting poet that closes it, Heaney has expanded the connotations of the phrase "moving the world," transforming it into one replete with the political implications that surround many of the poems from *North*. Among the emotions that order the poem, disillusionment reigns supreme—"unacknowledged" is an important word in Shelley's phrase, repudiating Milton's phrase, "fame is the spur." Anonymity in Shelley's scheme is the price paid for the gift of prophecy, but it ultimately provides the spur that goads the poet to pin his name to the poetry. Tarzan, as Heaney claims, also "shook the world"; Burrough's jungle-lord was the most hidebound pastoralist of the twentieth century, both in the original novels and the wildly nostalgic films that brought to armchair colonialists a comforting succession of Edenic jungles watched over by their ivory-skinned patron.

But aboriginal innocence supplies only half of the pastoral dream; the other half, the "insinuation," lies in commitment and commentary.

The second part of *North,* well known for its political, prosaically rendered verse, relies nonetheless on stock pastoral motifs in two of its central poems. Part two of "Singing School," a six-part poem, describes a constable's visit to Heaney's father; the constable, obviously English, has come to inquire about the crops grown by the poet's father. The poem begins and ends with a description of the policeman's bicycle, an image in the poem that ultimately approaches a metonymic level, so closely aligned is its mechanic efficiency with the policeman's character:

> He stood up, shifted the baton-case
>
> Further round on his belt,
> Closed the domesday book,
> Fitted his cap back with two hands,
> And looked at me as he said good-bye.
>
> A shadow bobbed in the window.
> He was snapping the carrier spring
> Over the ledger. His boot pushed off
> And the bicycle ticked, ticked, ticked.

Earlier in the poem, the poet's father had made his "tillage returns"; inquisition and guilt, bywords of the Catholic who lives in contemporary Northern Ireland, are first experienced by the boy within the rural context:

> I sat staring at the polished holster
> With its buttoned flap, the braid cord
> Looped into the revolver butt.
>
> 'Any other root crops?
> Mangolds? Marrowstems? Anything like that?'
> 'No.' But was there not a line
> Of turnips where the seed ran out
>
> In the potato field? I assumed
> Small guilts and sat
> Imagining the black hole in the barracks.

Mangolds and marrowstems grow in a garden responsible for one of the poet's earliest guilts, one of his clearest and most persecuting fears. The divisive distinctions between English and Irish, guilt and innocence, rural and urban, confrontation and subservience—all of these are suggested here by the poet's organization of the poem, an organization that reserves the central stanzas for the pastoral inset. The three stanzas that concentrate on the "root crops," particularly the one that fires the poet's "small guilts," lend these vegetables a political significance not often reserved for turnips. But Heaney is operating in the role of the implicator, one of the roles most familiar to the poet of the pasture, and as he rambles through his childhood memories, pausing here and there to tell a story, he displays the pastoralist's ability to endow the simplest rural detail with extensive implications: the poem not only records the meticulous aggressiveness of the Englishman with his "domesday book," it also chronicles the arrival of "small guilts," the original affliction of Edenic communities.

"Exposure," the last poem of "Singing School," begins in Wicklow where Heaney lived for four years after leaving Belfast in 1972. The move to the South occasioned a measure of criticism from the poet's community, and the poem views Heaney's cottage and the surrounding countryside as a retreat, a rural refuge from the troubles; in this sense, the poem is traditionally pastoral in its vision of the regenerative powers of life in the country:

> I am neither internee nor informer;
> An inner émigré, grown long-haired
> And thoughtful; a wood-kerne
>
> Escaped from the massacre,
> Taking protective colouring
> From bole and bark, feeling
> Every wind that blows. . . .

Prufrock had exclaimed, "I am not Prince Hamlet, nor was meant to be;/Am an attendant lord, one that will do/To swell a progress, start a scene or two. . . ." The syntactic pattern in the passage from Heaney's poem registers a similar note of diminished self-confidence—its confidence lies in denial. When Prufrock continues his monologue, he addresses subjects that have concerned Heaney as he considers the issue of a poet's political responsibility. Prufrock's mutterings aptly summarize the pandering foppishness that Heaney and all writers labeled political must fear:

> . . . no doubt, an easy tool,
> Deferential, glad to be of use,
> Politic, cautious, and meticulous;
> Full of high sentence, but a bit obtuse;
> At times, indeed, almost ridiculous—
> Almost, at times, the Fool.

Heaney, who has "escaped from the massacre," has also escaped from advising the Prince. He had written earlier in the poem that he found himself at Wicklow "weighing and weighing/[his] responsible *tristia*," and although the Republic of Ireland does not offer the severities of the Black Sea, echoes of an Ovidian crisis linger in the bitterness that rises from gossip and slander:

> How did I end up like this?
> I often think of my friends'
> Beautiful prismatic counselling
> And the anvil brains of some who hate me
>
> As I sit weighing and weighing
> My responsible *tristia*.
> For what? For the ear? For the people?
> For what is said behind-backs?

Ultimately, the sense of what Clare termed "rurallity" pervades this poem, endowing the countryside with the maternal, sustaining qualities that describe the traditional pastoral refuge, the retreat from the hustle and bustle of daily life that encourages philosophical detachment. This rendition represents a far more traditional aspect of pastoral writing than does Heaney's revisionary version of the Iron Age. Much of the poetry that follows "Exposure," the last poem of *North*, uses these pastoral themes and images as an informing background, and as background material, they often assume traditional guises.

As a result, brief insinuations recall well-developed traditions. Several poems from *Field Work* exhibit the kind of generic confidence that calls on a single pastoral image to consolidate the several governing ideas of a poem that would seem otherwise to have little to do with the genre. In "Oysters," which begins the collection, Heaney describes a gathering of friends on the coast. Eating oysters, they have come to lay down "a perfect memory/In the cool of thatch and crockery." But the shellfish, "alive and violated," dredge up memories of the plundering Romans who exported the oysters, "packed deep in hay and snow"; laboriously carried over the Alps, they ultimately arrived in Rome to be enjoyed by the Emperor. Such exploitation, innocuous as it may seem, encourages Heaney to hope that this meal, a kind of convivial Last Supper, "might quicken me all into verb, pure verb." The purity of Heaney's response to political suppression has always been derived from the purity of the language deployed to register that response—linguistic purity here refers to nothing more than what Heaney called the ability of any language to suggest "images and symbols adequate to our predicament."[1] For Heaney, nostalgia has its linguistic dimension, and it is called etymology. Again the subject of language dominates the poem. But a small detail in the phrasing suggests even more clearly a pastoral setting. To arrive at this feast, to participate in the banquet that would give rise to Heaney's observations, he "had driven to that coast/Through flowers and limestone." For an instant, it seems that he is moving through a field of flowers, that he is passing through a pastoral initiation to receive the wisdom bestowed on him—and the reader—at the end of the poem. Perfect memories, here laid down, might well become the stuff of nostalgia. Through the "flowers" and on to "pure verb," to the poet's brand of action: the poem quietly recreates the refining ritual that structures much pastoral poetry as it moves from a brief but pointed glimpse of the more perfect world to the harsher world of social, even political, commitment. Innocence, the pastoral illusion, urges commitment, the pastoral intention.

The poem immediately following "Oysters" reenforces this traditional vision of pastoral innocence and simplicity that begins to characterize Heaney's manipulation of the genre. The second part of *North* had suggested that Heaney might turn his eye to a new kind of realism, one that would confront the violence of his culture in ways less oblique than the imaginatively elaborate reconstructions of Iron Age rituals found in the earlier poems. The first section of "Tryptych" is entitled "After a Killing," and the plaintive simplicity of the subject's presentation further develops the characteristic tone of the last poems of *North:*

> There they were, as if our memory hatched them,
> As if the unquiet founders walked again;
> Two young men with rifles on the hill,
> Profane and bracing as their instruments.

> Who's sorry for our trouble?
> Who dreamt that we might dwell among ourselves
> In rain and scoured light and wind-dried stones?
> Basalt, blood, water, headstones, leeches.

Wordsworth's Lucy "dwelt among the untrodden ways," and the death recorded in that poem hangs like a shroud behind this one. The "rain and scoured light and wind-dried stones" recall the substantives, "the rocks and stones and trees" that situated Lucy within the "diurnal course" mentioned in "A Slumber Did My Spirit Seal." As Heaney's poem continues, he begins to daydream, thinking of "small-eyed survivor flowers,/The pined-for, unmolested orchid," a nostalgic and regenerative pastoral daydream whose consolations lie in distraction. Often in *Field Work,* the most brutal civil violence is described in the most traditionally pastoral terms. The peculiar safety inherent in an august literary genealogy reflects one of the governing emotions that the poet brings to the contemplation of his country's troubles: the desire for self-preservation.

The last stanza of the poem presents a simple resolution to the contradictory feelings that accompany the aftermath of a killing:

> And to-day a girl walks in home to us
> Carrying a basket full of new potatoes,
> Three tight green cabbages, and carrots
> With the tops and mould still fresh on them.

The poem ends factually with a simple report "of what happens," to borrow a line from "Song," another poem in *Field Work.* Yet the girl, fresh from the garden, arrives as the hyacinth girl arrived from her garden in "The Burial of the Dead," the first section of *The Waste Land;* there, the hyacinth girl had come with "[her] arms full, and [her] hair wet," and the speaker's "eyes failed" when confronted with her lush vigor. Heaney, more certain of his malady than the speaker of Eliot's poem, turns eagerly to the comforts offered by the girl who comes to him with her own garland. Her sudden appearance in the last stanza of the poem affords Heaney a renovating glimpse into a world of growth and fertility. Among the "wind-dried stones," her brimming abundance is out of place, and she provides a momentary resolution to the conflicting sorrows and emotions that gave rise to the poem. Such a resolution, because of its entrancing innocence and fertility, is as attractive as it is unattainable—the pastoral vision has always dealt in titillation, and that is why, never glutted by satisfaction, the poetry continually entices.

Enticement has long provided the pastoral with one of its definitive strategies, but the pastoral elegy, one of the tradition's most important family members, depends upon emotional sobriety. And such sobriety, both in Heaney's appropriation of the literary form and his assessment of the troubles, begins to dominate the poetry of *Field Work,* as it leaves behind the brash renovations of Denmark's bogs for the quieter pastures of the literary tradition. "The Strand at Lough Beg" is dedicated to Colum McCartney, one of Heaney's relatives, who as a note tells us, "was the victim of a random sectarian killing in the late summer of 1975." Much in this poem resists the eulogy and insists on the elegy, wondering with a journalist's curiosity what happened, "what," as Milton phrased it, "hard mishap hath doom'd this gentle swain?" And like Milton, whose defining horror was to think of King dying at sea, away from England, with his bones "wash[ed] far away," Heaney shows a similar insistence on imagining what actually happened. Milton's is the more sublime imagination, Heaney's the more exacting, but the fundamental concern is common to both poets:

> What blazed ahead of you? A faked road block?
> The red lamp swung, the sudden brakes and stalling
> Engine, voices, heads hooded and the cold-nosed gun?
> Or in your driving mirror, tailing headlights
> That pulled out suddenly and flagged you down
> Where you weren't known and far from what you knew:
> The lowland clays and waters of Lough Beg,
> Church Island's spire, its soft treeline of yew.

Speaking of his family, Heaney associates McCartney with the rural folk, the "Big-voiced scullions, herders, feelers round/Haycocks and hindquarter, talkers in byres,/Slow arbitrators of the burial ground." The poem turns on the single image of McCartney's cattle which now "graze/Up to their bellies in an early mist," an image of comfortable, almost hackneyed complacency. Seeing these cattle alive, as if still belonging to McCartney, Heaney envisions him coming "through squeaking sedge/Drowning in dew," and finally finds him on his knees, "With blood and roadside muck in [his] hair and eyes." No less curious is Milton about the

details of King's death, and no less ritualistic is Heaney concerning the
funeral procession:

> I . . . kneel in front of you in brimming grass
> And gather up cold handfuls of the dew
> To wash you, cousin. I dab you clean with moss
> Fine as the drizzle out of a low cloud.
> I lift you under the arms and lay you flat.
> With rushes that shoot green again, I plait
> Green scapulars to wear over your shroud.

Milton had called for "every flower that sad embroidery wears" to weave
the funeral wreath, "to strew the Laureate Hearse where Lycid lies," and
Heaney's plaited green scapulars serve a similar purpose. McCartney's
death is marked by a pastoral ritual—the native greenery of the land-
scape represents the hope of Irish regeneration that Heaney brings to bear
on the despair occasioned by the loss of a loved one.

Here, as in all pastoral elegy, the work of the poet—the plaiting of
the scapular—is an intimate part of the process of grieving; but literary
ploys, once they become sanctioned by a generic name, often seem far
removed from the emotional need that bred them. "The Strand at Lough
Beg" is governed by this pure spirit of authorship, of gauging the depth
of one's grief by the beauty of one's response, one's poem, to the loved
one. Funeral wreaths and plaited scapulars are the Miltonic equivalents
for the poem itself, and a fretful concern for its creation, for the strength
of its literary artifice, has always characterized the English elegiac
tradition. Although Milton's version of pastoral represented a radical
pastiche of elements classical, pagan, and Christian, "Lycidas" quickly
became a tradition in itself, a conserving haven for several important
pastoral images. Heaney's poetry, while attempting to address explicitly
the horrors of random killing in Northern Ireland, relies on essentially
conservative interpretations of the literature that informs his versions of
pastoral toward the end of the 1970s. The tension created between the
soothing strains of the old pastoral and the grimly insistent logic of
secular violence shows a new direction in his work, one less concerned
with generic innovation but more insistent on portraying the dire exigen-
cies of life in a beleaguered state.

Elegiac poetry often seems overly insistent on finding the resolving
image, the one that will best express the specific emotional matrix from

which both grief and consolation arise. And the poetry of *Field Work* often deploys the pastoral in similar ways. In a poem such as "High Summer," which chronicles the poet's departure from Wicklow, the final line of the final stanza holds out the promise of a redemptive memory, one that might glean from the poet's stay in the countryside the consolations that will strengthen him as he makes his way back to "the crossroads":

> We left by the high bare roads of the *pays basque*
> where cavalries sentry the crossroads like masts
> and slept that night near goatbells in the mists.

These "goatbells in the mists" recall the "cattle . . . in an early mist" appearing in "The Strand at Lough Beg." The bare roads guarded by cavalries cut an evil and urban swath by the tinkling goatbells of the misted pasture, the pasture where the poet, where every poet, passes the night. Both "High Summer" and "The Strand at Lough Beg" wear their pastoralism in ways more traditional than the poems of *North*. *Field Work,* however, if it occasionally dallies with the obvious contrasts of pastoral, also depends upon a saturating pastoral context, one that invests a rare and extensive confidence in the tradition. "The Toome Road" issues from an overarching sensibility broadly pastoral in its definitive contours:

> One morning early I met armoured cars
> In convoy, warbling along on powerful tyres,
> All camouflaged with broken alder branches,
> And headphoned soldiers standing up in turrets.
> How long were they approaching down my roads
> As if they owned them? The whole country was sleeping.
> I had rights-of-way, fields, cattle in my keeping,
> Tractors hitched to buckrakes in open sheds,
> Silos, chill gates, wet slates, the greens and reds
> Of outhouse roofs. Whom should I run to tell
> Among all of those with their back doors on the latch
> For the bringer of bad news, that small-hours visitant
> Who, by being expected, might be kept distant?

The village of Toome provided the title for a poem included in *Wintering Out.* It had begun, "My mouth holds round/the soft blastings,/*Toome,*

Toome," and it marked one of the early stages of Heaney's linguistic nostalgia, of his attempt to survey his childhood home and cordon it with a sense of privilege and magic. Pastoral writing, an inherently confrontational literature, often demanded an attractive otherworldliness from its localities. In "The Toome Road," the poet expresses his indignation at being invaded by this "warbling" convoy; it is as if the intruders, "camouflaged with broken alder branches," had disguised themselves to gain entrance into Toome, his private paradise—Calidore, arrayed in his "shephearde's weeds," also invaded a pastoral society, and in winning Pastorella's love he succeeded in his task.

The closing lines of the poem resort to overstatement, and an innocuous rhetoric governs the tone:

> O charioteers, above your dormant guns,
> It stands here still, stands vibrant as you pass,
> The invisible, untoppled omphalos.

The sense of the passage is clarified by the first paragraph of "Mossbawn," the opening essay of Heaney's prose collection, *Preoccupations:*

> I would begin with the Greek word, *omphalos,* meaning the navel, and hence the stone that marked the centre of the world, and repeat it, *omphalos, omphalos, omphalos,* until its blunt and falling music becomes the music of somebody pumping water at the pump outside our back door. It is County Derry in the early 1940s. . . . There the pump stands. . . . Five households drew water from it. . . . The horses came home to it in those first lengthening evenings of spring, and in a single draught emptied one bucket and then another as the man pumped and pumped, the plunger slugging up and down, *omphalos, omphalos, omphalos.*

The pump here is granted the Eliotic privilege of standing at the center, at the still point, of the turning world, but the parched horses do not belong to biblical prophets. They are most likely draft horses; the mantric chant Heaney associates with the farmer and his animals raises them to a level that could easily accommodate the need for the sacred, redemptive life, but in secular terms pastoral writing has often accommodated that need, and so it does here. In Heaney's hands, the pastoral dream of earthly perfection arises naturally from the invading tanks that spoil it; he preserves, without directly addressing, the thematic tension between the urban and the rural, the civilized and the uncivilized—between, ultimately, *us* and *them*—that has characterized the literature from its beginning.

As the poetry of *Field Work* tends less and less toward generic revision, traditional pastoral emotions appear and reappear, briefly linking the poem with old ways of categorizing the disparate elements of daily experience. By recreating certain situations and by placing certain characters within those situations, Heaney is able to fashion a poetry of the pastoral gesture. "September Song" recasts the ancient and commonplace attitudes towards the fall season, attitudes which reflect the ambivalence of a season known both for its bountiful harvests and its eroding decay. The poem even includes the shepherd's traditional answer to these changing fortunes; by the end of the passage, Heaney invokes the sympathetic powers of music:

> In the middle of the way
> under the wet of late September
> the ash tree flails,
> our dog is tearing earth beside the house.
>
> In rising ditches the fern subsides.
> Rain-logged berries and stones
> are rained upon, acorns
> shine from grassy verges every morning.
>
> And it's nearly over,
> our four years in the hedge-school.
> If nobody is going to resin a bow
> and test the grieving registers for joy
>
> we might as well put on our old record
> of John Field's *Nocturnes*. . . .

This is essentially a song of leave-taking, and Heaney relies for these set pieces on the pastoral nuance, the hint of detachment and perfection that gilds his landscape. The ambiguity of the season is reflected by the scene itself, the dog "tearing earth" and the acorns that "shine from grassy verges"; and the contraries outside of the house prepare for similar contraries inside of the house, where the poet will "test the grieving registers for joy," an accurately rendered jumble of emotions that confronted Milton in a similar season, when he faced his own "sad occasion dear." The poem ultimately moves to conclusions that do not depend on

pastoral solutions; but the poem embodies, as do many of the poems of
Field Work, a keenly honed pastoral sensibility, one that serves Heaney
in subtle but important ways.

This sensibility occasionally exhibits the inventive precision of the
seventeenth-century lyricist, particularly that of Andrew Marvell. Pas-
toral writing holds no franchise on the metaphysical conceit, but the
metaphysical conceit finds that pastoral writing offers a trove of possibil-
ities; in "Ametas and Thestylis Making Hay-Ropes," Marvell uses a
familiar rural image, the hay rope, to support an elaborate exposition of
desire:

I.

Ametas:

Think'st Thou that this Love can stand,
Whilst Thou still dost say me nay?
Love unpaid does soon disband:
Love binds Love as Hay binds Hay.

II.

Thestylis:

Think'st Thou that this Rope would twine
If we both should turn one way?
Where both parties so combine,
Neither Love will twist nor Hay.

III.

Ametas:

Thus you vain Excuses find,
Which your selve and us delay:
And Love tyes a Womans Mind
Looser then with Ropes of Hay.

IV.

Thestylis:

What you cannot constant hope
Must be taken as you may.

V.

Ametas:

Then let's both lay by our Rope,
And go kiss within the Hay.

As the age demands, Heaney's version of this pastoral love scene is at once less contrived and more realistically rendered than Marvell's brief epigrammatic piece, but its unusual tone, its ability to sustain the same kind of playful confidence of Marvell's poem, marks it as a legitimate heir. "The Harvest Bow," written in unobtrusive couplets, three to a stanza, is not a seduction piece and does not dwell exclusively, erotically, on the excitements of the present moment. The poem begins in recollection:

> As you plaited the harvest bow
> You implicated the mellowed silence in you
> In wheat that does not rust
> But brightens as it tightens twist by twist
> Into a knowable corona,
> A throwaway love-knot of straw.

The final three stanzas of the poem begin with the nostalgic vision of young love and end with a social decree, and the transition between the two depends upon the changing functions of the harvest bow:

> And if I spy into its golden loops
> I see us walk between the railway slopes
> Into an evening of long grass and midges,
> Blue smoke straight up, old beds and ploughs in hedges.
> An auction notice on an outhouse wall—
> You with a harvest bow in your lapel,
>
> Me with the fishing rod, already homesick
> For the big lift of these evenings, as your stick
> Whacking the tips off weeds and bushes
> Beats out of time, and beats, but flushes
> Nothing: that original townland
> Still tongue-tied in the straw tied by your hand.
>
> *The end of art is peace*
> Could be the motto of this frail device
> That I have pinned up on our deal dresser—
> Like a drawn snare
> Slipped lately by the spirit of the corn
> Yet burnished by its passage, and still warm.

The poem moves quickly from a narration of a past incident to a narration of a past incident *remembered*, from the narrative voice to the recollective voice; the evening recalled is one "of long grass and midges," and the poet is "already homesick/For the big lift of these evenings." Intensely personal, the memory triggered by the harvest bow engenders a less personal, more social pronouncement: *"The end of art is peace."* Perhaps this is a private peace, an individual contentment, but the aphoristic language suggests a wider significance for the maxim. Yet the emotions that lie behind that maxim, and that ultimately give rise to it, draw their strength from a past framed by the "golden loops" of the bow; such gildings, particularly when dealing with history—either personal or national—rely on a pastoral historiography that emphasizes the consoling perfections of the past.

The loops of the harvest bow stand in stark contrast to the torc tightened around the Tollund Man; the radical revisions of pastoral nostalgia that led Heaney to the Tollund Man's torc have been replaced by an acceptance of the tradition's standard symbols. Complacency often provides an occasion for indiscriminate acceptance, but Heaney's version of Wicklow, where he and his family lived for four years after leaving Belfast, descends from his version of the Irish Free State, the twenty-six counties lying south of Northern Ireland. The poems do not extol the political entity known as the Irish Republic; they offer, as traditional pastoral offers, an imaginative interlude, a consoling vision of the rural society that provides an attractive alternative to the life the poet flees. In this case, the political assignations of these two societies are English and Irish in their governments. But the nostalgia of the verse, while it seems to be innocuous in its ramblings, provides the foundation for a larger statement, a credo of sorts, that links the prosperity of art to the well-being, the peace, of the poet's society.

Marking a return to a more traditional verse form, the ten "Glanmore Sonnets" which fall near the middle of *Field Work* further develop the nostalgic strain and serve in one sense as a paean to County Wicklow. Heaney's pentameter, lush and ornately crafted, contrasts sharply with the clipped lines of the first section of *North;* and the imagery of the sonnets, their insistence on country matters, would seem to place the sonnets at a distance from the explicitly political concerns of the second section concluding *North.* But pastoral writing readily offers glimpses of the world beyond the pasture. Heaney, reflecting a pastoral sensibility almost classical in its lineaments, has called it a "teacherly notion" that "poems with rural or archaic images . . . aren't dealing with the modern world."[2] The ten sonnets, in fact, are very much about the modern world; and at the center of the sequence, at the center of the modern world envisioned by the poems, the fourth, fifth, and sixth sonnets offer an extended recollection of past times. But the first three sonnets of the sequence establish the conventional tone, the respectful cadences and images that characterize the work as a whole.

In his review of an anthology of pastoral verse, Heaney confessed that he "occasionally talked of the countryside where we live in Wicklow as being pastoral rather than rural, trying to impose notions of a beautified landscape on the word. . . ." Commenting on this, Morrison tells us that the poems of the sequence are "self-consciously pastoral right down to their 'classical' bay-tree and echoes of Horace and Virgil. Yet the sequence is not, as pastoral verse nowadays tends to be accused of being, either simplistic or escapist."[3] Overlying the entire sequence is a patina of contentment, a satisfaction with things as they are; and the first three sonnets speak of abundance and fertility. Heaney is portraying here the poet's retreat, one that would have interested Milton during his residence at Horton, and so fertility and abundance have their linguistic dimension. The subject of language figured prominently in Heaney's Iron Age poetry. In the octet of the first sonnet, the subject returns:

> Vowels ploughed into other: opened ground.
> The mildest February for twenty years
> Is mist bands over furrows, a deep no sound
> Vulnerable to distant gargling tractors.
> Our road is steaming, the turned-up acres breathe.
> Now the good life could be to cross a field
> And art a paradigm of earth new from the lathe
> Of ploughs. My lea is deeply tilled.

The poet stands poised at the instant before inspiration with his fallow imagination ready to give forth, while "old ploughsocks," as the poem continues, "gorge the subsoil of each sense." Heaney's metaphor for the creative process is brusquely constructed, and the sequence is given wholly, abruptly, to an investigation of the intricacies of poetic composition. How closely Heaney connects these pastoral images of fertility and abundance with the creative process is made clear by the closing lines of the sonnet:

> . . . Breasting the mist, in sower's aprons,
> My ghosts come striding into their spring stations.
> The dream grain whirls like freakish Easter snows.

On one level, the poem depicts Heaney's dream of fertility, a pastoral dream because it envisions County Wicklow as a place apart from other places, characterized by a "deep no sound." Yet like most enchanted lands, like the idealized gardens of the literature, it is susceptible to the sobering intrusions from the other, urban, outside world; it is "vulnerable to distant gargling tractors." The snows that end the poem and provide the pastoral antithesis to the "mildest February" that began the poem recall the snows that fall on Ireland, that fell "faintly through the universe," at the end of Joyce's story "The Dead." But Joyce's story is very much a story of Dublin's social life, a life experienced by finely drawn characters involved in finely drawn affairs. The world of this poem, although immensely attractive, even seductive, resides as all pastoral resides in the realm of the conditional—"the good life *could* be to cross a field" (emphasis added). The snow, the mists, the ghosts, and the whirling grain obscure the configuration of Wicklow's fields, and these spectral figures emphasize the poem's otherworldliness, its fantastic proportions. Traditional pastoral writing depended on this illusion, on this magical propensity, to make the contrast between the city and the country seem starkly drawn; here, Heaney's poem relies on similar divisions, yet does so with a distinctly modern idiom.

Of the ten sonnets that constitute the sequence, the second is the one most concerned with the subject of language, of how an individual poetic language is cultivated and nourished. The final couplet, with its highly patterned repetition of words and sounds, constructs the verbal analog for the activity it describes: "Vowels ploughed into other: open ground,/ Each verse returning like the plough turned round." Aside from repeating, with a slight syntactic difference, the opening line of the first sonnet, the couplet further identifies the cultivation of verse with the poet's arrival in the country, a land that offers him metaphors both for and about poetry. In the ninth line of the same sonnet, Heaney refers to Glanmore, where he lives in County Wicklow, as a "hedge-school," recalling the old Catholic hedge-schools organized in the nineteenth century before a formal education was permissible for Irish Catholics. Lessons were conducted beside the hedges and under the trees, and in this sonnet sequence, an archly English literary tradition, the mention of these "underground" schools strikes a note of resistance that has always found a sympathetic response in the structure of pastoral writing. In the third sonnet, Heaney parodies the pastoral gentility of the "uncommitted" life, and he wittily associates it with a measure and a poet distinctly English:

> This evening the cuckoo and the corncrake
> (So much, too much) consorted at twilight.
> It was all crepuscular and iambic.
> Out on the field a baby rabbit
> Took his bearings, and I knew the deer
> (I've seen them too from the window of the house,
> Like connoisseurs, inquisitive of air)
> Were careful under larch and May-green spruce.
> I had said earlier, 'I won't relapse
> From this strange loneliness I've brought us to.
> Dorothy and William—' She interrupts:
> 'You're not going to compare us two. . . ?'
> Outside a rustling and twig-combing breeze
> Refreshes and relents. Is cadences.

A cuckoo, a corncrake, deer, a baby rabbit, larch, and spruce, and all of these described as elements of a "strange loneliness"—it is difficult to imagine a more idealistic, more tranquil countryside. The "twig-combing breeze" blows across the twigs as it blew across the strings of Coleridge's Eolian harp, that quintessentially Romantic instrument. "The Eolian Harp" began in the garden of a cottage "o'ergrown/With white-flowered Jasmin, and the broad-leaved Myrtle,/(Meet emblems they of Innocence and Love!)," and Coleridge's garden too is sequestered from the world. The music of his harp makes a "soft floating witchery of sound/As twilight Elfins make, when they at eve/Voyage on gentle gales from Fairy-Land." And "honey-dropping flowers" grow here, a botanical perfection possible only in a pastoral setting. By the end of the third sonnet, Heaney has discovered a similar retreat in Wicklow, one that "refreshes and relents"; most importantly, he has cast himself in the role of the beleaguered poet who has fled to the country, and this posture, looking back to Tityrus's comfortable villa in the Italian countryside, is essentially pastoral.

But the English presence in this poem, both in its evocation of one of England's sainted poets and in its use of one of England's dominant verse forms, lingers ominously, and several poets have suggested that Heaney's muse has attempted to straddle the Irish Sea with one foot resting in London, the other in Dublin. Ciaran Carson, a young Irish poet, began the title poem to his volume, *The New Estate,* with four lines that read as if they were replying to the opening of Heaney's third sonnet:

> Forget the corncrake's elegy. Rusty
> Iambics that escaped your discipline
> Of shorn lawns, it is sustained by nature.
> It does not grieve for you, nor for itself.[4]

The sympathetic complicity of the natural world with the pastoralist—whether shepherd, farmer, or poet—seems an unnatural, deceiving complicity to Carson. The pathetic fallacy is an inherently civilizing but dominating convention because it immodestly assumes that nature reflects the poet's joys and sorrows. The soothing natural world of the third sonnet, when compared to the barbarous climates of *North,* does seem in Carson's word "shorn," even pared down in intensity. Such narcotic reticence, however nourishing, runs against the grain of the Republican spirit in Ireland, and this is as true in the matter of prosody as it is in the matter of politics. Even if Carson's poem does not intentionally respond to the world outlined in Heaney's poem, the poem nonetheless exhibits a distrust of the various kinds of Englishness that confront and confound the poet writing in the tradition labeled, almost antagonistically, Anglo-Irish. Pastoral comforts may entail political defections.

And so too may iambic pentameter. Anthony Easthope, in *Poetry as Discourse,* summarizes the many ideological implications that spring from the use of iambic pentameter, and although meter alone does not provide solid ground for political supposition, Easthope's comments on the iambic pentameter line elucidate an important aspect of Heaney's sonnet sequence, of his return to a traditional line organization following the clipped lines that characterized much of *North.* Speaking of the verse form during its "founding moment" in the Renaissance, Easthope observes that its name alone "reaches back to the quantitative metre of Greek and Latin" and that our native language, as it attempted to approximate the quantitative scheme of classical prosody, "is brought into relation with the classical model." To the uninitiated, the implications may seem dire: "So a particular practice of the national tongue can dress itself in the clothes of antiquity and a bourgeois national aspiration may represent itself in the form of universal civilization. The pentameter is favoured by the English court at the Renaissance. . . ."[5] In abandoning the harsh northern deities and the curtailed lines of *North* for the tutelary spirit of Wordsworth and the plush pentameters of *Field Work,* Heaney would seem in Easthope's terminology to lapse into a "bourgeois national aspiration"; and it is well known that his move to Wicklow was seen as a defection by some of his colleagues.

Ironically, however, Heaney resorts to a pastoral convention to resolve the subtleties of the problem. Childhood, or rather, an artful version of childhood's innocence, remoteness, and simplicity, fuels many nostalgic visions, and even Yeats, the promenading Irishman who claimed to remember "little of childhood but its pain," crowded the first chapter of his *Autobiography* with highly enameled recollections of Sligo, a place that he in fact rarely visited.[6] The fourth sonnet of the sequence alone represents the reconciliatory aspects of pastoral writing and supplies the thematic transition to the various versions of pastoral love that end the sequence. Heaney begins the fourth sonnet with a storyteller's verbal construction, one that, more often than not, signals the advent of a fond recollection:

> I used to lie with an ear to the line
> For that way, they said, there should come a sound
> Escaping ahead, an iron tune
> Of flange and piston pitched along the ground,
> But I never heard that. Always, instead,
> Struck couplings and shuntings two miles away
> Lifted over the woods. The head
> Of a horse swirled back from a gate, a grey
> Turnover of haunch and mane, and I'd look
> Up to the cutting where she'd soon appear.
> Two fields back, in the house, small ripples shook
> Across our drinking water
> (As they are shaking now across my heart)
> And vanished into where they seemed to start.

After the extensive aesthetic and domestic orientations of the first three sonnets—settling into the cottage and establishing the inspirational possibilities of rural seclusion—the fourth sonnet begins the middle section. Here, Heaney outlines a childhood experience that ultimately concerns an epistemological matter—how he might know for certain that a train was approaching. The conventional wisdom, introduced by the formulaic phrase, "they said," advised putting his head to the tracks to hear "the flange and piston pitched along the ground," a sound Heaney never heard. Instead, he watched "the head/Of a horse swirled back," and remarks that "two fields back," an innately rural way of giving directions, the drinking water shook with "small ripples." The horse and the water bucket are the harbingers that Heaney best understands because they are more personal, more intuitive, in kind than the humming tracks that intrude, like the "gargling tractors" of the first sonnet, on Heaney's home. The nationalistic, less personal nuances embedded in the second and third sonnets are answered by the intensely personal epistemology erected in the fourth. Faced with the political implications of his domestic exile, Heaney calls upon a childhood experience, a nostalgic vision, to assure him of his intuitive powers. Because they seem pristinely aboriginal, these intuitive powers provide a cogent response to the political conundrums plaguing both Heaney's life and his poetry. It is as if Heaney were searching for an unimpeachable authority, a place from which to begin again; and in this endeavor, Heaney, like most modern writers, inherits the Wordsworthian vision of childhood. These childlike methods of reasoning and learning were, at the very least, innocent of their responsibilities to the larger society, and when the political or social problems of that society weaken the writer's artistic convictions, the writer returns imaginatively to a time when such problems did not exist. Praising the intuitions of childhood is a nostalgic endeavor. Their priority, for the pastoral writer, argues for their persuasiveness.

The last three sonnets of the sequence resolve their several conflicts by resorting to the strengths and securities of love. In the eighth sonnet, the poet's country life continually reminds him of the other world, the world that the poet had left in Belfast:

> Thunderlight on the split logs: big raindrops
> At body heat and lush with omen
> Spattering dark on the hatchet iron.
> This morning when a magpie with jerky steps
> Inspected a horse asleep beside the wood
> I thought of dew on armour and carrion.
> What would I meet, blood-boltered, on the road?

"The Toome Road," a poem appearing earlier in *Field Work,* had begun with a similarly simple declaration: "One morning early I met armoured cars." In Wicklow, Heaney is far removed from the Toome road, but the conjunction of imagery is the same in both poems. The violent intrusion of the machinery is countered in the poem by the stubborn persistence of the natural world, a world which functions, when seen in contrast to these war machines, as the pastoral world. "The Toome Road" asserted an inviolable sense of place—"the visible, untoppled omphalos." But the eighth sonnet resorts now to other consolations, other comforts when the poet, presumably speaking to his wife, ends the poem with a note of quiet desperation:

> Do you remember that pension in *Les Landes*
> Where the old one rocked and rocked and rocked
> A mongol in her lap, to little songs?
> Come to me quick, I am upstairs shaking.
> My all of you birchwood in lightning.

The cryptically phrased last line recalls the first line where light from thunder had illuminated the split logs. This combination of impersonal, Heraclitan elements, of earth and fire, is transformed suddenly at the end of the poem into an image of the purely personal dimension. Perhaps it is too banal to suggest that Heaney's marriage represents an enduring consolation to the political problems suggested by the "armour and carrion" in the poem; the conflagration, intense and inflammatory, of the last line defines another experience, another area of Heaney's life that might compensate for the cataclysmic social changes of his community.

The final poem of the sequence revolves around a dream and ultimately proposes an erotic resolution to the various tensions of the poem. The interjection of the ninth line is taken from Wyatt's "They Flee from Me," a poem whose sense of erotic intrigue informs Heaney's poem. In a besieged country, the poet dreams a version of the pastoral dream, as he and his lover sleep "on a moss in Donegal":

> And in that dream I dreamt—how like you this?—
> Our first night years ago in that hotel
> When you came with your deliberate kiss
> To raise us towards the lovely and painful
> Covenants of flesh; our separateness;
> The respite in our dewy dreaming faces.

The respite here is of no political consequence; by the end of the sequence, the woes of the world have been momentarily put aside for the pleasures of a personal relationship. In the penultimate sonnet, however, the peculiar powers of such a relationship loom even larger in the pastoral context:

> Outside the kitchen window a black rat
> Sways on the briar like infected fruit:
> 'It looked me through, it stared me out, I'm not
> Imagining things. Go you out to it.'
> Did we come to the wilderness for this?
> We have our burnished bay tree at the gate,
> Classical, hung with the reek of silage
> From the next farm tart-leafed as inwit.
> Blood on a pitch-fork, blood on chaff and hay,
> Rats speared in the sweat and dust of threshing—
> What is my apology for poetry?
> The empty briar is swishing
> When I come down, and beyond, your face
> Haunts like a new moon glimpsed through tangled glass.

The major themes are here—the pastoral gentility of the "burnished bay tree" set against the tooth and claw of nature's "infected fruit"; the active life as seen in "the sweat and dust of threshing" juxtaposed with the contemplative life glimpsed in an "apology for poetry"; and the seclusion of the "wilderness" which suggests in this context its opposite, the political engagement of life in Belfast. The poem addresses the sources and responsibilities of poetry, a theme which underlies much pastoral writing, and the final couplet of the poem offers a brooding response to the question that precedes it, a solution given to the intimate comforts of a personal relationship.

As the radical pastorals of *North* were designed to develop the larger racial concerns of the verse, the more conservative pastoral elements of *Field Work* emphasize the more personal, domestic concerns of the poet. The "tangled glass" of the last line of the ninth sonnet suggests the blurred focus, the inevitable distortions that complicate these relationships, but the "face/ . . . like a new moon" seen through that glass promises certain rewards for enduring, for attempting to see through those distortions. A new feeling of intimacy governs these poems, and the etymology of the word *intimacy*—the Latin adjectival root "intimus" means innermost—implicates the values of the inner life. Nourished by the pastoral seclusion in Wicklow, the inner life yields for Heaney a peculiar wisdom, one that seems, when buffeted by the parade of public images found in much of his poetry—the tanks, the cars, the soldiers, the guns—pared down and perhaps unequal to the grand tasks often expected of his work. Yet, as the sequence indicates, the small world of personal affairs, with its compromises, questions, and gratifications, is structurally analogous to the large world of political affairs, with its treaties, interrogations, and rewards. Ultimately it provides the basis for the poetry written from his seclusion, his pastoral retreat.

The sonnet sequence, with its emphasis on domestic affairs, contrasts with the genealogical concerns of the Iron Age poems. Yet the progression from the racial family to the immediate family is orderly and understandable. In these later poems, Heaney's hearth assumes the importance of Denmark's fens, and both of them serve as altars of sorts, places to which Heaney repairs for understanding and rejuvenation. As a subject for poetry, however, hearths are less spectacular than fens, particularly fens that continually deliver such startling corpses, eels, and quernstones. The "Glanmore Sonnets," while they represent the end of Heaney's retreat from the overtly political to the intimately familial, also yield his fullest assessment of the relationship between these two poles. The poems of *Field Work* were composed just after Heaney had written his review on the anthology of pastoral verse, a review where he had wondered if various themes and images of twentieth-century writing were not "still occasionally continuous with the tradition." He certainly had his own sonnets in mind. His willingness to view the essential themes of the tradition as the vital remnants of the tradition provide an effective model for reading and understanding the several appearances of pastoral in his later work.

Many of the poems in *Station Island* are suffused with a sensibility that draws on vestiges of pastoral imagery to structure the poetry. But no longer will whole sections of the volume depend upon the tradition; it is as if pastoral sentiments erupt sporadically, serve their purpose, and return to a kind of dormancy, awaiting their next appearance. But such unscheduled appearances have their own value as well—Heaney's gradual abandonment of pastoral schemes and strategies must loom large in any assessment of his overall accomplishment. Several poems from *Station Island* seem to dally with the old themes without embracing them. The fourth section of "Shelf Life" is entitled "Iron Spike," and its insistent curiosity about New Hampshire in the "age of steam" gives birth to an exotic rendition of the past, one whose "grassy silent path" hints at the kind of pastoral seclusion of the "Glanmore Sonnets":

So like a harrow pin
I hear harness creaks and the click
of stones in a ploughed-up field.
But it was the age of steam

at Eagle Pond, New Hampshire,
when this rusted spike I found there
was aimed and drive in
to fix a cog on the line.

What guarantees things keeping
if a railway can be lifted
like a long briar out of ditch growth?
I felt I had come on myself

in the grassy silent path
where I drew the iron like a thorn
or a word I had thought my own
out of a stranger's mouth.

And the sledge-head that sank it
with a last opaque report
deep into the creosoted
sleeper, where is that?

And the sweat-cured haft?
Ask the ones on the buggy,
Inaudible and upright
and sped along without shadows.

Mistaking the iron spike, a relic from the industrial age, for a harrow pin, an implement from the pre-industrial age, Heaney falls prey to the pastoral fallacy: harrow pins and iron spikes, both of which seem so similar in appearance, represent entirely different cultures, yet Heaney's immediate response to the object—a kind of Rorschach test—reveals his particular set of presumptions, his definitive obsessions. Heaney was not wrong to hear "harness creaks" when he saw the railroad spike; the "harness creaks," the noises of a simpler time, are never far from the governing music of his imagination.

The landscape of Heaney's latest work is haunted by characters who exhibit in one way or another a vital relationship to the past, and often these characters become for him an extension of that landscape, bearing on their clothes the grasses, seeds, and blossoms of the countryside. The Tollund man had carried "winter seeds" in his stomach; the man in "Last Look" wears them on his shirt sleeves. The entire poem is worth quoting because it shows how forcefully Heaney's imagination is carried from the present situation of the poem to an idealizing reminiscence of the past, a past which shows a pastoral lineage:

> We came upon him, stilled
> and oblivious,
> gazing into a field
> of blossoming potatoes,
> his trouser bottoms wet
> and flecked with grass seed.
> Crowned blunt-headed weeds
> that flourished in the verge
> flailed against the car
> but he seemed not to hear
> in his long watchfulness
> by the clifftop fuchsias.
>
> He paid no heed that day,
> no more than if he were
> sheep's wool on barbed wire
> or an old lock of hay
> combed from a passing load
> by a bush in the roadside.
>
> He was back in his twenties,
> travelling Donegal
> in the grocery cart
> of *Gallagher and Son,*
> *Merchant, Publican,*
> *Retail and Import.*
> Flourbags, nosebags, buckets
> of water for the horse
> in every whitewashed yard.
> Drama between hedges
> if he met a Model Ford.

> If Niamh had ridden up
> to make the wide strand sweet
> with inviting Irish,
> weaving among hoofbeats
> and hoofmarks on the wet
> dazzle and blaze,
> I think not even she
> could have drawn him out
> from the covert of his gaze.

When Heaney first finds the old man, he seems an integral part of the pasture he surveys, and Heaney's comparison of him to "sheep's wool" and a "lock of hay" emphasizes his role in the poem as an indigenous spirit, a *genius loci*. Through this mechanism, Heaney's poem returns to a perfected past of rural abundance with "flourbags, nosebags, buckets/ of water for the horse/in every whitewashed yard." Intractable, detached, even perhaps stubbornly antiquated, the man nontheless endures; his dreams are those of a simpler time, and they are informed by a traditional pastoral nostalgia, one which Heaney deploys sparingly but cunningly in the poetry of *Field Work* and *Station Island*. If the old man's country is beset by civil and political turmoil, the poem bears no record of it. But the renovating pastoral vision always issues from the need for renovation, and the poet's imagination, having struggled to reconcile the barbarity of his northern ancestors in the Iron Age poems, seems unavoidably drawn to the charmed simplicity of the man in the pasture, a man who in Heaney's retelling becomes an emblem for the untrammeled Celtic sensibility that once united the country.

Thomas Hardy is the subject of "The Birthplace," and even in a poem conceived partly in homage to the novelist, a familiar set of images appears, images that draw briefly and succinctly on the pastoral vision of sexuality in Arcadia:

> That day, we were like one
> of his troubled pairs, speechless
> until he spoke for them,
>
> haunters of silence at noon
> in a deep lane that was sexual
> with ferns and butterflies,

scared at our hurt,
throat-sick, heat-struck, driven
into the damp-floored wood

where we made an episode
of ourselves, unforgettable,
unmentionable,

and broke out again like cattle
through bushes, wet and raised,
only yards from the house.

The poem, in the third section, turns to a meditation on the poet's past
and its conjunction with the novelist's work:

Still, was it thirty years ago
I read until first light

for the first time, to finish
The Return of the Native?
The corncrake in the aftergrass

verified himself, and I heard
roosters and dogs, the very same
as if he had written them.

The "troubled pairs" of the second section compare Heaney and his
lover to the ill-fated couples of Hardy's novels, most obviously, perhaps,
at this stage of the poem, to Tess. The beautiful landscapes of the Wessex
countryside in *Tess of the D'Urbervilles* provided the sobering back-
ground for the grotesque labors of the people who lived there, a narrative
technique that owes much to antipastoral literature. But Tess's primordial
sexuality often found its equivalent in the lush groves that were her
natural habitat, and several vignettes from the novel seethe with an
Arcadian sensuality. The second section of Heaney's poem, which has
the satiated lovers rejuvenated, "wet and raised," imagines the place of
their tryst as a place "sexual/with ferns and butterflies." Here is the
bower of Hardy's pastoral, one that insists on the erotic aspect of inno-
cence, and in Heaney's version, hidden, as the lovers are, in the "deep
lane," a feeling of reassurance lingers in the lovers' fulfillment, a feeling

which, in the final section, is echoed by the poet's assurance that things in the world are as Hardy described them: "I heard/roosters and dogs, the very same/as if he had written them." The world of Hardy's pastoral is verified by the pastoral of Heaney's world.

Throughout the poems of *Station Island* lie glimpses of themes that had warranted more extensive development in the earlier poetry. The subject of language, from the study of etymology to the recreation of dialectal rhythms in his verse, has always remained in the foreground of Heaney's poetry. His Iron Age poetry embodies a linguistic nostalgia with distinctively pastoral implications: Heaney, as if looking back to a past Golden Age, plunders a word's history, attempting to locate the original valences that might illuminate a historical continuity between the violence of contemporary Northern Ireland and the Iron Age of Denmark. This fascination with language, with its hidden secrets, persists in his latest poetry. "The Loaning" begins by combining several elements that recur throughout Heaney's various versions of pastoral:

> As I went down the loaning
> the wind shifting in the hedge was like
> an old one's whistling speech. And I knew
> I was in the limbo of lost words.
>
> They had flown there from raftered sheds and crossroads,
> from the shelter of gable ends and turned-up carts.
> I saw them streaming out of birch-white throats
> and fluttering above iron bedsteads
> until the soul would leave the body.

By the end of the poem, this "limbo of lost words" will become associated with Dante; in this poem, the word "hedge," as in the "Glanmore Sonnets," speaks of the indomitable spirit responsible for the hedge-schools of Ireland. Heaney has again entered the realm of "lost words," the realm perhaps of those Irish words, like Dedalus's "tundish," not represented in the dictionary but nonetheless a vital part of the language that Heaney, like Dedalus, heard as a child. The second section develops this linguistic nostalgia; here, however, it has nothing to do with etymology:

> Big voices in the womanless kitchen.
> They never lit a lamp in the summertime
> but took the twilight as it came

like solemn trees. They sat on in the dark
with their pipes red in their mouths, the talk come down
to *Aye* and *Aye* again and, when the dog shifted,
a curt *There boy!* I closed my eyes
to make the light motes stream behind them
and my head went airy, my chair rode
high and low among branches and the wind
stirred up a rookery in the next long *Aye*.

This brief, finely etched vignette is charged with the joys of simple recollection, of recalling those childhood moments that appear, as age advances, to derive their power from the conversations, the individual expressions that distinguished them. For Heaney these verbal nuances are restorative. The third section opens with a kind of musical perfection:

Stand still. You can hear
everything going on. High-tension cables
singing above cattle, tractors, barking dogs,
juggernauts changing gear a mile away.
And always the surface noise of the earth
you didn't know you'd heard till a twig snapped
and a blackbird's startled volubility
stopped short.

The second half of this section addresses other issues within other contexts as Heaney speaks of those times when "you are tired or terrified/[and] your voice slips back into its old first place." The poem, with its "interrogator [who] steels his *introibo,*" becomes more overtly political in its diction. Each of its three sections, however, begins with careful descriptions of the sounds associated with three rural scenes. The beginning of the third section, with the imperative to "Stand still. You can hear/everything going on," suggests the music of the sphere, a music that ultimately expresses the most profound order of the universe. But for Heaney this is a dream of an idealized language because the poem ends with the sickening "click of a cell lock." The poem had begun in "the loaning," a right-of-way, where "the wind shifting in the hedge was like/an old one's whistling speech." Here is the "limbo/of lost words," words that had come to rest in the loaning from "raftered sheds and crossroads,/from the shelter of gable ends and turned-up carts." The language described in the section haunts the neglected or abandoned places of the countryside, and its recovery, the ultimate intention of this poem, represents another version, more darkly resolved, of Heaney's linguistic nostalgia. This dream of an idealized language is a purifying dream, and it reenacts the essentially pastoral desire of all flute-playing shepherds to sing and play the perfect song, the one whose melody, because it so elegantly extends an ancient tradition, wins the golden bowl.

Heaney's poetry has rarely been a predictable poetry; from book to book, the developing style, the obsessing subjects, continue in a gradual course of refinement. That is a matter of aesthetic continuity. It is not surprising, though, to find in *Station Island* several poems that recapture the pastoral's defining spirit, the spirit that Kermode described thus: "The first condition of pastoral poetry is that there should be a sharp difference between two ways of life, the rustic and the urban. The city is an artificial product, and the pastoral poet invariably lives in it, or is the product of its schools and universities. Considerable animosity may exist between the townsman and the countryman."[7] Having carried out his extensive revisions of the pastoral sensibility in the earlier books, Heaney, in "Changes," allows this first condition to provide the structural logic for his poetry:

> As you came with me in silence
> to the pump in the long grass
>
> I heard much that you could not hear:
> the bite of the spade that sank it,
>
> the slithering and grumble
> as the mason mixed his mortar,
>
> and the women coming with white buckets
> like flashes on their ruffled wings.

In "Iron Spike," the poet had heard "harness creaks" while walking on an old railway line. But that meditation had ended with a sense of transcience and loss. When "Changes" continues, Heaney follows another direction, one that completes Kermode's first condition:

> The cast-iron rims of the lid
> clinked as I uncovered it,

something stirred in its mouth.
I had a bird's eye view of a bird,

finch-green, speckly white,
nesting on dry leaves, flattened, still,

suffering the light.
So I roofed the citadel

as gently as I could, and told you
and you gently unroofed it

but where was the bird now?
There was a single egg, pebbly white,

and in the rusted bend of the spout
tail feathers splayed and sat tight.

So tender, I said, "Remember this.
It will be good for you to retrace this path

when you have grown away and stand at last
at the very centre of the empty city."

The carefully tended egg, the fondly remembered rural home—Heaney's ability to create and sustain an analogy accounts for much of his skill as a pastoralist. The advice given at the end of the poem, while it acknowledges the dichotomy between the "centre of the empty city" and the "citadel" with the incubating bird, does so as if such schisms were an unavoidable condition of the times. The pastoral world that lingers in the background of this book seems as remote as the bird perched in the well, and this distance between the city and the country has always characterized the literature. But the tone of this poem is paternal, and although no textual evidence supports the claim, the poem seems to recall an incident with a child. The last lines perhaps are advice given to a son or a daughter. As an arbitrator, as a father, Heaney commends to the child's memory the sustaining image that metaphorically nourishes all pastoral writing, that of "the single egg, pebbly white," sequestered from the world and gleaming in its detachment.

Even though such a poem faithfully preserves Kermode's first condition of pastoral writing, the tendency to accept that condition without argument or revision is new to Heaney's work. The militarized landscapes of *Death of a Naturalist,* the ferocious nostalgia of the Iron Age poems, and even the deftly political insinuations of the "Glanmore Sonnets" do not predict the quiet resignation of this poem. Perhaps the title, "Changes," provides the warning. But there is a deeper ambivalence in Heaney's work, an ambivalence that concerns the nature of the literary enterprise. Heaney has always been suspicious of his occupation as a writer, and he makes careful distinctions when describing his rural ancestors—they were not illiterate, he claimed in his interview with John Haffenden, they were simply not literary. Such vigorous skepticism tempers his poetry. But it also accounts for his peculiar perspective as a pastoral writer. More and more, Heaney is becoming the arbitrator, assuming the role of mediator between the two cultures he precariously straddles. The particular evolution of pastoral verse allowed it, as Puttenham demonstrated, to insinuate and glance at other subjects, and this flexibility provided Heaney with the vehicle to attempt such mediations. "Making Strange," examined earlier, becomes one of the poems most concerned with the precarious balance Heaney has maintained in his career between a rural childhood and an urban education. It is in fact emblematic of the larger cultural, social, and political mediations attempted by much of his verse. The poet has returned to his rural homeland and introduces one of his more "travelled" friends to a local resident:

> I stood between them,
> the one with his travelled intelligence
> and tawny containment,
> his speech like the twang of a bowstring,
>
> and another, unshorn and bewildered
> in the tubs of his wellingtons,
> smiling at me for help,
> faced with this stranger I'd brought him.
>
> Then a cunning middle voice
> came out of the field across the road
> saying, 'Be adept and be dialect,
> tell of this wind coming past the zinc hut,

call me sweetbriar after the rain
or snowberries cooled in the fog.
But love the cut of this travelled one
and call me also the cornfield of Boaz.

Go beyond what's reliable
in all that keeps pleading and pleading,
these eyes and puddles and stones,
and recollect how bold you were

when I visited you first
with departures you cannot go back on.'
A chaffinch flicked from an ash and next thing
I found myself driving the stranger

through my own country, adept
at dialect, reciting my pride
in all that I knew, that began to make strange
at the same recitation.

Essentially, the poem encourages Heaney to refurbish the dialectal rhythms that first "visited" him, while loving "the cut of this travelled one." Yet the poem ends on a note of pride as the poet drives his traveled friend through his "own country." If Heaney had not heard the encouraging speech from the "middle voice," he would have been ashamed to begin such a tour.

But this is a simplification of the poem. Pastoral literature happily assumes Janus's mask, and like Sir Calidore in Arcadia, pastoral characters show a clear ability to move in sustained secrecy among unfamiliar communities. In "Making Strange" Heaney is fooling no one, nor is he attempting any sort of masquerade—standing "between them," Heaney stands between the silent culture that nourishes his verse and the articulate culture that appreciates it. Pastoral literature, because it traditionally opposed one way of life with another, values the mediator, the shepherds from Thrace whose rhetorical skills make them a valuable commodity in a poem written for an audience living in Alexandria. The "cunning middle voice" that comes to Heaney grants him these mediational powers, and with incredible, accusing faces on either side of the poet, it arrives in the nick of time. Much of Heaney's work attempts this kind of reconciliation between antagonistic inflections, dictions, perspectives, cultures, and, ultimately, nations. Unlike the pastoral writer who suddenly found his dream of Arcadia spoiled by the noise from the street, Heaney is continually "making strange," forcing himself to revise the old notions, the habitual ideas about Ireland that transform persuasive visions into brittle dreams. In each poem, as he prepares to make strange, to introduce to the pastoral tradition another version, another Irish latecomer, he stands, with slight peril and much dexterity, between those visions and dreams.

Epilogue

On March 1, 1981, Bobby Sands began the hunger strike that would end with his death, sixty-six days later on May 5. During the three months that followed, nine others died of starvation in the Maze Prison, and the world's attention was drawn to the endurance of those who daily willed their deaths, ostensibly in pursuit of five prison reforms. In this case, the spirit of reform bequeathed to many Irish Republicans the harshly restorative legacy of martyrdom. "The myth of redemptive sacrifice," as Padraig O'Malley has written, "hardened and held."[1] But the redemption offered by the sacrifice often exacts its toll in guilt and diffidence. How can a lifetime's cloistered devotion to the composition of verses, wonders the poet from Northern Ireland, justify itself in the face of such dire social and political exigency?

In the twelve-part title poem of *Station Island,* Heaney confronts the ghosts from his past, one of whom, his second cousin, Colum Mc-Cartney, was murdered by Protestants. In the poem, McCartney knows of yet another poem that Heaney had written *in memoriam* and included in his previous collection, *Field Work.* "The Strand at Lough Beg," which had ended with the poet plaiting "green scapulars to wear over your [McCartney's] shroud," represents a contemporary renovation of the pastoral elegy, and in part eight of "Station Island," McCartney responds to the enervation felt by Heaney at the news of McCartney's death:

'You saw that, and you wrote that—not the fact.
You confused evasion and artistic tact.
The Protestant who shot me through the head
I accuse directly, but indirectly, you
who now atone perhaps upon this bed
for the way you whitewashed ugliness and drew
the lovely blinds of the *Purgatorio*
and saccharined my death with morning dew.'

To confuse evasion with artistic tact, to sweeten violence and death with the sympathetic metaphor—these are the ploys of traditional pastoral, and they recall the *modus operandi* of Johnson's censures against "Lycidas." Investigating the relation between the artistic imperative and the political conscience, Heaney allows one of his characters to indict his own poetic method, and in doing so, embraces the traditional skepticism that originally brought disfavor to pastoral writing. Much of Heaney's recent poetry, in abandoning pastoral strategy, has taken as its subject matter the theoretical issues that pastoral poetry was originally intended to solve, or at least, circumvent. And one of the signal subjects of the genre, from Virgil's political eclogues, through Milton's religious elegy, to Crabbe's scathing couplets, has been that of social responsibility.

McCartney's renunciation of "The Strand at Lough Beg" issues from the confessional that houses all of those writers continually called on to confront the reality, as it is often labeled, of life in a troubled society. For the artist, the dangers of self-indulgence continually threaten the integrity of the individual vision that would remain responsible to the culture that nourished it. The terms of this responsibility have always engaged Heaney in his prose, and since the poem "Exposure"—the last poem of "Singing School," which ends *North*—his poetry too has become increasingly concerned to analyze the problem of social responsibility. In a recent essay on Sorley Maclean, a Gaelic poet, Heaney remarked that he found many of Maclean's verses to be "sustenance and example to somebody undergoing his own uneases about the way a poet should conduct himself at a moment of public crisis." His analysis of these "uneases" has taken many forms, but none are so graphic as his poetic representations of the extreme violence in several parts of "Station Island." In the seventh section, for example, Heaney faces the ghost of an old college friend who was shot in his shop by terrorists. When Heaney sees him, his head is "blown open above the eye," and blood has dried "on his neck and cheek." After the man relays the story of his murder, Heaney pleads, "Forgive the way I have lived indifferent— /forgive my timid circumspect involvement. . . ." In her review of *Station Island,* Helen Vendler helpfully identifies the three faces of Heaney's "self-portrait" as "sometimes the abashed apprentice. . . , sometimes the guilty survivor. . . , sometimes the penitent turning on himself with hallucinatory self-laceration."[2] It is the "guilty survivor" here that begs forgiveness for a life of "timid, circumspect involvement." The comfortable sacrifices of the literary life pale to insignificance beside the extreme exactions of random killing.

Such comparisons never seem irrelevant to writers who are forced to make them. Vendler locates the self-lacerating penitent in section nine of "Station Island" where in a dream Heaney speaks of his "blanching self-disgust." And again, as in sections seven and eight, Heaney is asking forgiveness for what is here termed the "unweaned life that kept me competent/To sleepwalk with connivance and mistrust." More important than Heaney's self-laceration, however, is the cause of his anguished penitence. The section had begun with the monologue of a hunger striker, now dead:

'My brain dried like spread turf, my stomach
Shrank to a cinder and tightened and cracked.
Often I was dogs on my own track
Of blood on wet grass that I could have licked.
Under the prison blanket, an ambush
Stillness I felt safe in settled round me.
Street lights came on in small town, the bomb flash
Came before the sound, I saw country
I knew from Glenshane down to Toome
And heard a car I could make out years away
With me in the back of it like a white-faced groom,
A hit-man on the brink, emptied and deadly.
When the police yielded my coffin, I was light
As my head took aim.'

American readers often underestimate the thoroughgoing influence exerted by the ordeal that began in September 1976, when Kieran Nugent went "on the blanket" in the Maze Prison, a phrase echoed in the fifth line of the monologue and one that refers to the refusal by Nugent, and eventually by many other prisoners, to wear prison clothing. Instead of the standard uniform, the protesting prisoners, most of them Irish Republicans, wore only their prison blankets. By 1978, the Loyalists who had originally joined the protest gave up their stand because the movement had become so closely aligned with Republican sentiment. And in October 1980, seven prisoners began a hunger strike that would end after fifty-three days, when it appeared that a compromise with the British government was imminent. But negotiations ultimately faltered, and Bobby Sands refused food on March 1, 1981. The frustration, doubt, and guilt registered by the various sections of "Station Island" reflect the frustrations, doubts, and guilts of the Catholic population of Northern Ireland in the early 1980s when these poems were written and when the effects of the hunger strikes were most pervasive.

O'Malley has ascribed the extraordinary legacy of the hunger strikers to their enactment within their society of a "metaphysical ritual" which served as an "atonement for the mutilations, the meaningless maimings, the innumerable futile brutalities, and the hundreds of violent and misdirected deaths sanctioned in the name of holy nationalism." In fact, one of the recognized results of Northern Ireland's Republican movement involves the "prison culture." O'Malley succinctly describes its structure: "For every prisoner there are mothers, fathers, brothers, sisters, wives, children, networks of friends and relatives who feed off the prison culture, adopting its values, sharing its ethos, and cultivating its resentments, their perceptions of reality mirroring and often magnifying the perceptions of the prisoners themselves." When such extreme conditions become part of the daily fabric of society, the poet is more likely to ponder the relation between the poem and the condition. In his essay "The Noble Rider and the Sound of Words," Wallace Stevens spoke of "the pressure of reality," a phrase that he used variously to describe the traditional dichotomy between the internal world of imaginative vigor and the external world of daily affairs. One sentence in particular succinctly encapsulates the problem faced by the Irish writer of the early 1980s: "But when one is trying to think of a whole generation and of a world at war, and trying at the same time to see what is happening to the imagination, particularly if one believes that that is what matters most, the plainest statement of what is happening can easily appear to be an affectation."[3] Political activists and fighting soldiers, whatever their sins, are never inactive, and their healthy degree of practical zeal periodically raises a measure of envy and doubt in the sedentary poet. And for the poet from Northern Ireland, these envies and doubts are apt to infiltrate the most unlikely poems. Much of the self-questioning in Heaney's recent verse of this decade stems from his attempt to reconcile the world of letters and the world of political action, a reconciliation that strikes to the heart of pastoral literature.

Heaney's quandary over the role of the poet in times of civil unrest would more naturally engage one whose verse had participated in the pastoral tradition where the poetry's "highest concerns"—the "greater matters" that Puttenham spoke of in 1589—are always implied. But as Heaney's slain cousin reminded him, artistic tact is often the partner to evasion. In his most recent poetry, pastoral imagery and technique have been predictably replaced by the theoretical skepticisms that would hasten such a decline. Often, Heaney briefly recapitulates former scenes or situations that recall the old techniques and, as if disheartened by their diminished powers, dismisses them. In the fifth section of *Station Island*, Heaney confronts the ghost of Barney Murphy, his schoolmaster at the Anahorish School. In the brief lyric "Anahorish," included in *Wintering Out*, Heaney had originally described the region as " 'the place of clear water,'/the first hill in the world." When Heaney remarks that "you'd have thought that Anahorish School/was purgatory enough for any man," Murphy responds with a description that reveals how the resplendent innocence once associated with the place has faded:

> Then a little trembling happened and his breath
> rushed the air softly as scythes in his lost meadows.
> 'Birch trees have overgrown Leitrim Moss,
> dairy herds are grazing where the school was
> and the school garden's loose black mould is grass.'
> He was gone with that and I was faced wrong way
> into more pilgrims absorbed in this exercise.

As with McCartney's implied renunciations of Heaney's pastoral excesses, so Murphy's glum version of Anahorish continues the movement in Heaney's poetry away from the easy sympathy and concordant hope engendered by his early pristine landscapes. When faced with the enormity of sectarian violence in Northern Ireland, Heaney suggests here that a poetic method, even one as flexible as his own version of pastoral, can very quickly become an institution unto itself, and hence incapable of the cultural confrontations and revisions that characterized his earlier work.

Yet Heaney's unrest is not an occupational one, and his guilts, his "uneases," are ultimately assuaged by his own defense of poetry, which, rather than occupy him in one essay, has been scattered throughout several pieces collected under the title, *The Government of the Tongue*

(1988). In the prefatory essay, "Nero, Chekhov's Cognac and a Knocker," Heaney cites Nero's maniacal concert given while Rome burned as the "archetypal" example of the irresponsible artist, only to reverse the direction of his argument with the question, "Why should the joyful affirmation of music and poetry ever constitute an affront to life?" Here is Heaney the confirmed lyricist; and when confronted with the extreme example of Wilfred Owen, here is Heaney the skeptical lyricist: "Owen so stood by what he wrote that he seemed almost to obliterate the line between art and life: what we might call his sanctity is a field of force which deflects anything as privileged as literary criticism. . . . They so opt for truth that the beauty consideration is made to seem irrelevant." Earlier in the essay, Heaney had characterized the final twelve lines of "Dulce et Decorum Est" as a "violent assault . . . upon the genteel citadel of English pastoral verse," an indication that the term "pastoral" represents for Heaney a poetic perspective, one of safety and illusion, as much as it does a trove of imagery and metaphor. Heaney speaks of the problems that he confronted while presenting this poem to his students, and when he called their attention to the possibility of the last section being overwritten, he was forced to recognize "the immense disparity between the nit-picking criticism I was conducting on the poem and the heavy price, in terms of emotional and physical suffering, the poet paid in order to bring it into being."[4] The disparity between the artistic rendition and the life rendered, as we have seen throughout this study and as Heaney indicates in his revealing comment on "Dulce et Decorum Est," directly concerns pastoral writing. When successful, the literature has been called richly implicative, when unsuccessful, coldly artificial.

Throughout the essay, Heaney refers to several Eastern-bloc writers, and he is plainly aware of the affinities between them—"I keep returning to them because there is something in their situation that makes them attractive to a reader whose formative experience has been largely Irish." Heaney continues: "There is an unsettled aspect to the different worlds they inhabit, and one of the challenges they face is to survive amphibiously, in the realm of 'the times' and the realm of their moral and artistic self-respect, a challenge immediately recognizable to anyone who has lived with the awful and demeaning facts of Northern Ireland's history over the last couple of decades."[5] The events of these decades have aggravated the dichotomy between "the times" and "artistic self-respect," a dichotomy always present but most obviously offering itself as a credible subject matter only in times of extreme civil duress. That pastoral verse comes specially equipped to address these subjects is evident from Heaney's deft revision of the tradition; that he is now relying less and less on these techniques while concentrating once again on the problems those techniques were originally mustered to address is evident from the often exotic poetry of *The Haw Lantern*.

Delivered as one of the T. S. Eliot Memorial Lectures and included in *The Government of the Tongue*, "Sounding Auden" represents Heaney's attempt to locate precisely Auden's field of force—a phrase Heaney is fond of using when referring to a poet's inalienable and idiosyncratic inflection. Heaney is concerned to investigate the relation between Auden's authority and Auden's music, and although his assessments of the work generally reflect the common opinion that Auden's *music* gradually diminished in its revisionary boldness, Heaney's fine insights into Auden's work often point toward the literary precedents that shape the distinctive spirit of *The Haw Lantern*. Heaney selects the opening lines from two of Auden's famous early poems, quotes them, and appends beneath each one his own candid response:

> Who stands, the crux left of the watershed,
> On the wet road between the chafing
> grass . . .
> > *Between grass? What do you*
> > *mean? Where is this anyway?*
> Taller to-day, we remember similar evenings,
> Walking together in the windless orchard . . .
> > *Taller what? Whose orchard*
> > *where?*[6]

The opening lines of "The Mud Vision," one of the final poems of *The Haw Lantern,* invite a similar choral response from the reader:

> Statues with exposed hearts and barbed-wire crowns
> Still stood in alcoves, hares flitted beneath
> The dozing bellies of jets, our menu-writers
> And punks with aerosol sprays held their own
> With the best of them . . .
> > *Statues and alcoves? Where? The*
> > *best of them? Who?*

The tone of the poem—casual, slangy, presumptuous, yet fired by an offhand eloquence—recalls Auden's "In Praise of Limestone," not only in its echo of "the best and worst of us," but also in its sibylline

impenetrability. Both poems admit the conversational caesura—Auden's
is "my dear," and Heaney's "of course"—and both deploy the camp
tactic of relaying cataclysmic news with urbane indifference.

Characterizing Auden's method in the early poetry, Heaney has
characterized a stylistic feature of "The Mud Vision":

> This new lyric was dominated by a somewhat impersonal pronoun
> which enclosed much that was fabulous, passional and occasionally
> obscure. Its manifestations were an 'I,' or 'we' or 'you' which could
> arrest, confuse and inspect the reader all at once. He or she seemed to
> have been set down in the middle of a cold landscape, blindfolded,
> turned rapidly around, unblindfolded, ordered to march and to make
> sense of every ominous thing encountered from there on. The new
> poem turned the reader into an accomplice, unaccountably bound to
> the poem's presiding voice by an insinuation that they shared a knowl-
> edge which might be either shameful or subversive.[7]

Heaney's poem, although obscure in its references, presses its readers
toward a sympathetic familiarity with its viewpoint, one that allows its
participants to claim that "you could say that we survived." Heaney's
poetry has typically nourished a situational clarity—speakers are identi-
fied, conflicts detailed, and resolutions attempted. But in "The Mud
Vision" Heaney is insinuating, much in the manner of "In Praise of
Limestone," and the knowledge shared between speaker and reader is an
experiential knowledge, hard-won by wearied questers:

> We lived, of course, to learn the folly of that.
> One day it was gone and the east gable
> Where its trembling corolla had balanced
> Was starkly a ruin again, with dandelions
> Blowing high up on the ledges, and moss
> That slumbered on through its increase.

The "it" referred to here is the "mud vision/ . . . a gossamer wheel/Of
nebulous dirt." But a calamity ensues, a calamity of the memory, and the
familiar rhythms of freedom and confinement, of sovereignty and sup-
pression, are reestablished:

> Just like that, we forgot that the vision was ours,
> Our one chance to know the incomparable
> And dive to a future. What might have been origin
> We dissipated in news.

The familiar notes of recent Northern Irish history are sounded, but they are shorn of specificity, freeing them from their locale. Heaney is creating perspective, and inasmuch as the angle of observation is recognizable, it matters little that there are no bogs, bombs, or barbed-wire to specify time and place. The reader is transformed, as Heaney said of Auden's poetry, into "an accomplice," an ideological accomplice— comprehension of the poem relies on the reader's ability to locate and assume the intellectual perspective developed by the poem, a task neither aided nor waylaid by recognizable descriptions of recognizable places. The *paysage moralisé,* one of Auden's characteristic frameworks, is new in Heaney's work, and although it retains the pastoral emphasis on the politicized landscape, it does so within an entirely new tradition.

The spirit of this tradition is closely related to the spirit governed, as Auden claimed, by Ariel, the tutelary broker of poetry's power to enchant, proffering as it does so the illusion of order and harmony. In his essay, Heaney recognizes the ideological and theological aspects of Auden's career, but he wants, using Geoffrey Grigson as a model, to concentrate on the "music" of Auden's verse because "a new rhythm, after all, is a new life given to the world, a resuscitation not just of the ear but of the springs of being." In music, particularly new music, lie ideas, and it is the "hymn-singing effect of poetry, its action as a dissolver of differences," that offers, sometimes undeservedly, a degree of consolation. Concerning this strain in Auden's verse, Heaney writes:

> A poem floats adjacent to, parallel to, the historical moment. What happens to us as readers when we board the poem depends upon the kind of relation it displays towards our historical life. Most often, the relation is placatory and palliative, and the poem massages rather than ruffles our sense of what it is to be alive in experience. The usual poem keeps faith with the way we talk at the table, even more with the way we have heard other poems talk to us before. "Out on the lawn I lie in bed,/Vega conspicuous overhead/In the windless nights of June." Yes, Yes, we think; more, more; it's lovely, keep it coming. The melody allays anxiety. . . .[8]

Some of the new verse in *The Haw Lantern* "allays anxiety" in this special, rhythmic way, but its relation to the "historical life" is no less serious, no less considered, than the more obviously meditative poems of pastoral aspiration.

The situation of "Song of the Bullets"—the stars and planets shining brightly, the poet gazing intently—recalls Auden's "A Summer

Evening," the anxiety-allaying lyric that had engaged Heaney in his essay on Auden, and it provides further evidence of Auden's presence in *The Haw Lantern*. But "Song of the Bullets" owes a deeper debt to Auden's "As I Walked Out One Evening." Like Auden's poem, Heaney's deploys the ballad stanza and revolves around a song that appears within the body of the poem. The song, sung by lovers in Auden's poem, commences at the end of the second stanza:

> As I walked out one evening,
>> Walking down Bristol Street,
> The crowds upon the pavement
>> Were fields of harvest wheat.
>
> And down by the brimming river
>> I heard a lover sing
> Under an arch of the railway:
>> 'Love has no ending. . . .'

The song continues with the lover's declaration of steadfast devotion to the other and ends with Time incanting the lessons of *memento mori*. Heaney's lyric, which depends upon the reader hearing Auden's stately cadences, includes a song as well, but one sung by bullets:

> I watched a long time in the yard
>> The usual stars, the still
> And seemly planets, lantern-bright
>> Above our darkened hill.
>
> And then a star that moved, I thought,
>> For something moved indeed
> Up from behind the massed skyline
>> At ardent silent speed
>
> And when it reached the zenith, cut
>> Across the curving path
> Of a second light that swung up like
>> A scythe-point through its swathe.
>
> 'The sky at night is full of us,'
>> Now one began to sing,
> 'Our slugs of lead lie cold and dead,
>> Our trace is on the wing. . . .'

Auden's poem had ended as "the deep river ran on," but the second bullet in Heaney's poem declares that even "Mount Olivet's beatitudes" cannot overcome the "steady eye that ever/Narrowed, sighted, paused," a lyric recognition of the assassin's line of sight. Rivers do not run on at the end of Heaney's ballad; in fact, the only semblance of continuity and cosmic order—the stars and planets of the first stanza—has vanished by the last stanza:

> Now wind was blowing through the yard.
> Clouds blanked the stars. The still
> And seemly planets disappeared
> Above our darkened hill.

The accomplishment of the poem lies in its grim revision of Auden's sober, measured celebration of human mortality. The song sung by Auden's lovers is intensified by the poem's insistence on their mortality, and the metronomic inevitability of the verse reflects as surely the permanence of love as it does finally the inevitability of death. But Heaney's poem moves toward an equally complex synthesis of the lyric voice and the historical moment, one of the primary concerns of pastoral verse. Auden's "music" had originally been Heaney's concern; here in Heaney's own responsive music, the meter, mimicking the ideals of order, tolls in oppressive regularity, sounding a measure that refuses to allay the reader's anxiety—the poem ends on a "darkened hill." Anxious readers, chilled by the calm assurance with which the bullets foretell their dominion, must listen longer and more carefully to the resisting strains of the music that call into play the balladic tradition. In that tradition, whether in the hands of Anon. or Auden or Heaney, the song remains a simple testimony to the human outcry, to the joys and perfections of musical organization. "Lyric poetry," Heaney reminds us in his prefatory essay to *The Government of the Tongue*, "always has an element of the untrammelled about it," and even when the bullets sing, they have the presence of mind to sing in forceful, patterned numbers. Heaney has consistently developed this untrammelled voice in his own verse, and as his methods have evolved, departing from an essentially pastoral technique, he has continued to assert the primacy of his art's larger social responsibilities, preserving an essentially pastoral obsession.

Notes

NOTES FOR PREFACE

1. This essay, originally appearing in *The Listener,* was reprinted in Heaney's first collection of prose, *Preoccupations* (New York: Farrar, Straus, and Giroux, 1980) 30.

2. Tom Paulin, *The Faber Book of Political Verse* (London: Faber and Faber, 1986) 18.

3. Seamus Heaney, "The Indefatigable Hoof-taps," *The Times Literary Supplement* 5–11 Feb. 1988: 144.

4. Theodor Adorno, *Aesthetic Theory* (New York: Routledge and Kegan Paul, 1984) 7.

NOTES FOR CHAPTER I

1. All references to Heaney's poetry are taken from the following editions: *Death of a Naturalist, Door into the Dark, Wintering Out,* and *North* from *Collected Poems* (New York: Farrar, Straus and Giroux, 1980), *Field Work* (New York: Farrar, Straus and Giroux, 1979), *Station Island* (New York: Farrar, Straus and Giroux, 1985), *The Haw Lantern* (New York: Farrar, Straus and Giroux, 1987).

2. Samuel Johnson, "Pastoral Poetry, 2," *The Rambler,* 37, 24 July 1750. Reprinted in *Samuel Johnson,* The Oxford Authors, ed. Donald Greene (New York: Oxford University Press, 1984), 196–197.

3. "Discourse on Pastoral Poetry," in *The Prose Works of Alexander Pope,* ed. Norman Ault (Oxford: Basil Blackwell, 1936), 299.

4. Seamus Heaney, "An Open Letter," (Derry: Field Day Theatre Company, 1983), 9.

5. Richard Poirier, *The Renewal of Literature: Emersonian Reflections* (New York: Random House, 1987), 112.

6. Tom Paulin, "A New Look at the Language Question," Field Day Pamphlets, no. 1 (Derry: Field Day Theatre Company, 1983), 17.

7. William Empson, *Some Versions of Pastoral* (Norfolk, Connecticut; New Directions, 1950), 8.

8. Seamus Heaney, "In the Country of Convention: English Pastoral Verse," in *Preoccupations* (New York: Farrar, Straus, and Giroux, 1980), 173.

9. Ibid., 180.

10. John F. Lynen, *The Pastoral Art of Robert Frost* (New Haven: Yale University Press, 1960), 14.

11. Andrew Ettin, *Literature and the Pastoral* (New Haven: Yale University Press, 1984), 22.

12. Harold Toliver, *Pastoral Forms and Attitudes* (Berkeley: University of California Press, 1984), vii.

13. Virgil, *The Pastoral Poems,* ed. E. V. Rieu, (Middlesex: Penguin Books, 1972), 26. The translations are my own.

14. Raymond Williams, *The Country and the City* (New York: Oxford University Press, 1973), 26.

15. Seamus Heaney, "Belfast," in *Preoccupations,* 30.

16. Tom Paulin, introduction, *Political Verse,* 18.

17. George Crabbe, *Poems,* ed. Adolphus William Ward (Cambridge: Cambridge University Press, 1905), 121.

18. Heaney, "The Sense of Place," 131, 136.

19. James Randall, "An Interview with Seamus Heaney," *Ploughshares* 5 (1979) 3:14.

20. Patrick Kavanaugh, *Collected Poems* (New York: W. W. Norton, 1973), 34.

21. John Haffenden, *Viewpoints: Poets in Conversation with John Haffenden* (London: Faber and Faber Limited, 1981), 65.

22. *John Clare,* The Oxford Authors, ed. Eric Robinson and David Powell (New York: Oxford University Press, 1984), 153. Unless otherwise noted, all quotations from Clare's work are taken from this edition.

23. Seamus Heaney, "In the Country of Convention," 180.

24. *John Clare,* 153.

25. Ibid., 159.

26. Heaney, "Feeling into Words," *Preoccupations,* 43.

27. Haffenden, *Viewpoints,* 63.

28. Seamus Heaney, "A Poet's Childhood," *The Listener* (November 1971): 660; Frank Kermode, ed. *English Pastoral Poetry from the Beginnings to Marvell: An Anthology* (New York: W. W. Norton, 1972), 14.

29. George Saintsbury, *A History of English Prosody* (New York: Russell and Russell, 1961), 1, 229–30.

NOTES FOR CHAPTER 2

1. "Country of Convention," 179–80.

2. Seamus Heaney, "Mossbawn," *Preoccupations,* 20.

3. Paulin, "New Look at the Language Question," 5.

4. *The Poems of W. B. Yeats,* ed. Richard J. Finneran (New York: Mac-Millan Publishing Co., 1983), 7; Heaney, "Country of Convention," 180.

5. J. W. Tibble and Anne Tibble, *John Clare: A Life* (London: Michael Joseph, 1972), 99–100.

6. Ibid., 141.

7. Ibid., 142.

8. Seamus Heaney, "Forked Tongues, Ceilies and Incubators," *Fortnight* (September 1983): 18–19.

9. Laurence Lerner, *The Uses of Nostalgia* (London: Chatto and Windus Ltd., 1972), 44.

10. Tibble and Tibble, 52.

11. Lerner, *Uses of Nostalgia,* 44.

12. See, for example, Randall, "Interview with Seamus Heaney" or Haffenden, *Viewpoints,* 57 ff.

13. Haffenden, *Viewpoints,* 73–74.

14. Blake Morrison, *Seamus Heaney,* Methuen Contemporary Writers Series (New York: Methuen, 1982), 18 ff.

15. Anthony Easthope, *Poetry as Discourse* (New York: Methuen, 1983), 64; Haffenden, *Viewpoints,* 74.

16. John Wilson Foster, "Seamus Heaney's 'A Lough Neagh Sequence' ": Sources and Motifs," *Eire-Ireland* 12 (Summer 1977): 138.

17. Clare, *Oxford Authors,* 459.

18. Richard Fallis, *The Irish Renaissance* (Syracuse: Syracuse University Press, 1977), 256.

19. Randall, "Interview with Seamus Heaney," 7, 8.

20. Seamus Heaney, "The Impact of Translation," *The Yale Review* 76 (Autumn 1986): 3–4.

21. T. S. Eliot, "The Social Function of Poetry," *On Poets and Poetry* (London: Faber and Faber Limited, 1957), 22.

22. Ibid., 27.

23. Ibid., 20; Michael Hamburger, "Absolute Poetry and Absolute Politics," reprinted in *Poetry and Politics,* ed. Richard Jones (New York: Quill, 1985) 91.

24. Eliot, "Social Function of Poetry," 27, 28.

25. Seamus Heaney, "Feeling Into Words," *Preoccupations,* 56–57.

26. Morrison, *Seamus Heaney,* 17.

27. Seamus Heaney, "Out of London: Ulster's Troubles," *The New States-man* 72 (July 1966): 23.

28. Ibid., 24.

29. Ibid., 23.

NOTES FOR CHAPTER 3

1. Lerner, *Uses of Nostalgia,* 41.

2. Randall, "Interview with Seamus Heaney," 18.

3. Lerner, *Uses of Nostalgia,* 49.

4. Morrison, *Seamus Heaney,* 65.

5. John Braidwood, "Ulster and Elizabethan English," *Ulster Dialects: A Symposium,* ed. G. B. Adams (Holywood: Ulster Folk Museum, 1964), 46.

6. Randall, "Interview with Seamus Heaney," 19.

7. Patrick Kavanagh, *Tarry Flynn* (New York: The Devin-Adair Com-pany, 1949), 19–20.

8. James Joyce, *A Portrait of the Artist as a Young Man,* Centennial Edition (New York: The Viking Press, 1982), 188.

9. Seamus Heaney, "Out of London," 23.

10. Morrison, *Seamus Heaney,* 58–59.

11. Seamus Heaney, "Country of Convention," 180.

12. This version of "The Lament of Swordy Well" is taken from John Barrell's and John Bull's *English Pastoral Verse* (Penguin, 1974), the anthology reviewed by Heaney.

13. Edna Longley, "*North:* 'Inner Émigré' or 'Artful Voyeur,' " *The Art of Seamus Heaney,* ed. Tony Curtis (Bridgend, Mid Glamorgan: Poetry Wales Press, 1982), 76.

NOTES FOR CHAPTER 4

1. Seamus Heaney, "Feeling into Words," 56.

2. Haffenden, *Viewpoints,* 66.

3. Heaney, "Country of Convention," 173; Blake Morrison, *Seamus Heaney,* 85.

4. Ciaran Carson, *The New Estate* (Belfast: Blackstaff Press, 1976).

5. Anthony Easthope, *Poetry as Discourse,* 65.

6. *The Autobiography of William Butler Yeats* (New York: MacMillan, 1965), 5.

7. Frank Kermode, ed. *English Pastoral Poetry,* 14.

NOTES FOR EPILOGUE

1. Padraig O'Malley, *The Uncivil Wars: Ireland Today* (Boston: Hough-ton Mifflin, 1983), 266. The prisoners, 265 n., asked to wear their own clothes;

to refrain from prison work; to associate freely with one another; to organize recreational facilities and to have one letter, visit, and parcel a week; and to have lost remission time restored.

2. Seamus Heaney, "The Voice of a Bard," *Antaeus* 60 (Spring 1988): 298; Helen Vendler, *The Music of What Happens: Poems, Poets, Critics* (Cambridge: Harvard University Press, 1988), 162; originally published in *The New Yorker,* September 23, 1985.

3. O'Malley, *The Uncivil Wars,* 267, 272; Wallace Stevens, *The Necessary Angel: Essays on Reality and the Imagination* (New York: Vintage, 1951), 20.

4. Seamus Heaney, *The Government of the Tongue: The 1986 T. S. Eliot Memorial Lectures and Other Critical Writings* (London: Faber, 1988), xii, xiv xv.

5. Ibid., xx.

6. Ibid., 118.

7. Ibid., 117.

8. Ibid., 120, 121.

9. Heaney, *The Government of the Tongue,* xii.

10. Heaney, *The Government of the Tongue,* xiv.

Index

A Note about the Author

Sidney Burris received his B.A. in Latin and Classical History from Duke University where he later returned for post-graduate work in Greek. He spent one year at the University of Vienna, Austria, studying German language and literature, and then completed the M.A. and Ph.D. in English at the University of Virginia. He has received several fellowships and awards, including the Associated Writing Program's Anniversary Award for Poetry and the Academy of American Poets Prize. His first collection of poetry, *A Day at the Races,* won the University of Utah Press Poetry Award and appeared in June, 1989. His essays and poems have appeared in *Poetry, The Atlantic, Kenyon Review, Sewanee Review, Virginia Quarterly Review, Southern Review, NER/BLQ, Contemporary Literary Criticism,* and other places. He is currently Assistant Professor of English at the University of Arkansas.